Persuasive Signs

Approaches to Applied Semiotics
4

Mouton de Gruyter
Berlin · New York

Persuasive Signs

The Semiotics of Advertising

by
Ron Beasley
Marcel Danesi

Mouton de Gruyter
Berlin · New York 2002

Mouton de Gruyter (formerly Mouton, The Hague)
is a Division of Walter de Gruyter GmbH & Co. KG, Berlin

⊗ Printed on acid-free paper which falls within the guidelines
of the ANSI to ensure permanence and durability.

Library of Congress — Cataloging-in-Publication Data

Beasley, Ron, 1945—
   Persuasive signs : the semiotics of advertising / by Ron Beas-
ley, Marcel Danesi.
     p. cm. — (Approaches to applied semiotics ; 4)
   Includes bibliographical references and index.
   ISBN 3 11 017340 9 (cloth : alk. paper)
   ISBN 3 11 017341 7 (pbk. : alk. paper)
     1. Advertising.   2. Signs and symbols   3. Semiotics.
  I. Danesi, Marcel, 1946—   II. Title.   III. Series.
  HF5823 .B3725 2002
  659.1'01'4—dc21
                                            2002029569

Die Deutsche Bibliothek — Cataloging-in-Publication Data

Beasley, Ron:
Persuasive signs : the semiotics of advertising / by Ron Beasley ;
Marcel Danesi. — Berlin ; New York : Mouton de Gruyter, 2002
  (Approaches to applied semiotics ; 4)
  ISBN 3-11-017341-7
  ISBN 3-11-017340-9

Preface

The messages of advertisers are everywhere. They are on billboards, on the radio, on television, on buses and subways, in magazines and newspapers, on flyers, on clothes, shoes, hats, pens, and the list could go on and on. To say that advertising has become a ubiquitous form of mass communication in today's "global culture" is an understatement. Using both verbal and nonverbal techniques to make its messages as persuasive as possible, advertising has become an integral category of modern-day social discourse designed to influence attitudes and lifestyle behaviors by covertly suggesting how we can best satisfy our innermost urges and aspirations through consumption. As the American author E. B. White (1899–1985) aptly observed, in 1936, in a *New Yorker* article (11 July): "Advertisers are the interpreters of our dreams - Joseph interpreting for Pharaoh. Like the movies, they infect the routine futility of our days with purposeful adventure. Their weapons are our weaknesses: fear, ambition, illness, pride, selfishness, desire, ignorance. And these weapons must be kept as bright as a sword."

Given its obvious importance to understanding modern forms of expression, representation, and communication, it is little wonder that advertising has come under the microscopes of virtually all the cognitive and social sciences over the last fifty or so years. Indeed, the number of articles, books, and websites devoted to the critique, analysis, and/or discussion of advertising has become truly mind-boggling. The field of *semiotics*, too, has been extremely active in stimulating interest among semioticians, advertisers, and the public at large in the various signifying aspects of advertising. So, another semiotic work on this "over-studied" topic would seem to be needless, if not irrelevant, to increasing our understanding of advertising as a form of persuasive rhetoric. But, a closer look at the vast literature in this domain reveals that there exist, surprisingly, very few in-depth treatments of the actual persuasion techniques employed by the advertising profession to generate its ever-elusive meanings. And, to the best of our knowledge, few *textbook* treatments of advertising from the semiotic perspective - if any - are currently available. By writing this textbook, our goal has been to fill this conspicuous lacuna.

As in other fields of criticism - literary, musical, artistic, etc. - a work on advertising is bound to be highly reflective of the views and analytical preferences of its authors. This book is no exception. To get different, complementary, or supplementary views of advertising the reader is advised to consult the relevant works listed at the back of this book. Having issued this caveat, we wish to assure the reader that we have made every attempt possible to emphasize *method of analysis*, rather than our personal opinions. In our view, it is this exposition of method that the reader will hopefully find usable in various ways. This volume is intended as a textbook on how to carry out a coherent semiotic analysis of advertising. It is a book that many of our students and colleagues in the field have asked us to write. We have taken their suggestion to heart and directed our textbook towards: (1) a general audience interested in what semiotics has to say about advertising; (2) students taking introductory university courses in such areas as semiotics, communication theory, media studies, psychology, and culture studies; and (3) students enrolled in high school and college programs that prepare them for careers in advertising, marketing, or the media. We have written it, therefore, so that as broad an audience as possible can appreciate and understand, in a clear and practical way, how semiotic inquiry can be applied to the study of advertising. For this reason, both the style and contents of the book are tailored specifically for those without prior technical knowledge of the field. An appendix containing practical exercises is added for pedagogical uses of this textbook - either for classroom or personal study and practice. A convenient glossary of technical terms is also included at the end, as is a bibliography of suggested readings for more intensive study. In our view, there is perhaps no other domain of application like advertising that best shows the power of semiotics as a "science of interpretation."

The simple plan of this textbook is as follows. The opening chapter provides an overview of advertising as a form of social discourse, i.e. as an intrinsic component of how people understand and interact with each other in modern-day consumerist cultures. It starts with a schematic history of advertising, passing on to an initial explication of semiotic axioms and notions in this domain of inquiry. The second and third chapters constitute descriptions and applications of semiotic concepts to the study of all aspects of product advertising (brand naming, logo creation, etc.). Chapter II deals with the basic representational techniques that are used to generate a product's image, as well as the fundamental strategies employed to enhance product recognizability through various media and ad campaigns. Chapter III looks at the techniques used to imbue brand image, ads and commercials with connotative meanings. Both chapters are based on actual case studies in which the authors of this book have been involved. One of the authors is a professional marketer-advertiser (Ron Beasley); the other is an academic (Marcel Danesi). The final chapter constitutes our own reflections on the relation between advertising and contemporary culture, and especially on the effects that advertising is purported to have on the contemporary human psyche. Nowhere in the text are print ads used, as is the practice in textbooks, for two reasons: (1) it is difficult and expensive to reproduce them in all their colorful details; and (2) it has been virtually impossible to obtain permission from the manufacturers or advertising firms responsible for the ones we had chosen for inclusion. This has emphasized upon us how overly sensitive advertisers have now become to public opinion. Even those firms for whom we had worked prior to writing this book have been reluctant to give us the required authorization to use their print materials for illustrative purposes. However, this should in no way detract from the overall presentation of the subject matter. Moreover, print advertising is only one component of advertising textuality and, since the whole profession is characterized by rapid change, chances are that by the time this book goes to press, the images it would contain would already be *passé*.

As mentioned, the theoretical stances put forward and the analytical techniques illustrated throughout this text reflect our own approach to semiotics and our own interpretations of specific advertisements and product personalities. But whether the reader agrees or disagrees with any of our semiotic analyses is besides the point of this textbook. Our hope is simply that it will induce a perspective on advertising that he or she might not have had previously.

We wish to thank Victoria College of the University of Toronto for having allowed one of the authors the privilege of teaching in, and coordinating, its *Program in Semiotics and Communication Theory* over the past two decades. We also must thank the many students who, over the years, have been involved in collecting advertising materials and providing us with their own thoughts on the messages concealed within them. There are too many to mention here. However, of these, the following merit special mention: Adriana De Marco, Janet Winger, Marcus Sagar, Marianna Calamia, Mina Wallin, Thania Valle, Andrea Minicucci, Laura Shintani, Mandy Chima, Avi Braz, Angela De Luca, and Sandy Di Martino. These students have been instrumental in collecting the appropriate materials, and subsequently in helping us analyze them for the purposes of this book. We also must express our gratitude to the many colleagues who have given us a great deal of input over the years, both at professional conferences and through correspondence. Among these, the following deserve special mention: Jean Umiker-Sebeok, Leonard Sbrocchi, Paul Perron, Paul Cobley, Eero Tarasti, Frank Nuessel, Linda Rogers, Susan Petrilli, Augusto Ponzio, Patrizia Violi, Peter Schulz, Eddo Rigotti, Kalevi Kull, Peeter Torop, Myrdene Anderson, Lucia Santaella Braga, Winfried Nöth, and Don Cunningham. Last, but not least, a special debt of gratitude is owed to the late Professor Thomas A. Sebeok, Distinguished Professor at Indiana University, Honorary Fellow of Victoria College (University of Toronto), and Adjunct Professor of the Culture, Communications, and Information Technology Program of Erindale College of the University of Toronto for the unwavering support he always gave to our project, inviting us to submit it to his prestigious new series in applied semiotics. It is his intellectual influence that has shaped the study of semiotics in classrooms throughout this continent, and particularly, in our own classrooms. This book is dedicated to his memory.

Contents

Chapter III Creating textuality 95

Chapter I
Advertising as social discourse

I have discovered the most exciting, the most arduous literary form of all, the most difficult to master, the most pregnant in curious possibilities. I mean the advertisement. It is far easier to write ten passably effective Sonnets, good enough to take in the not too inquiring critic, than one effective advertisement that will take in a few thousand of the uncritical buying public.

Aldous Huxley (1894–1963)

1. Introductory remarks

The term *advertising* comes down to us from the medieval Latin verb *advertere* "to direct one's attention to." In line with its etymology, it can be defined simply as any type or form of public announcement intended to direct people's attention to the availability, qualities, and/or cost of specific commodities or services. The central idea behind modern-day advertising is that the appeal and salability of any product or service that is promoted in the marketplace, even in the most rudimentary fashion, are greatly enhanced. The craft of advertising today has, however, progressed considerably beyond the use of simple techniques for announcing the availability of products or services. It has ventured, in fact, into the domain of persuasion, and its rhetorical categories have become omnipresent in contemporary *social discourse* - i.e. in the content and delivery of the meanings that people living in a society exchange on a daily basis.

The messages of advertising have, as anyone can literally see, permeated the entire cultural landscape. Printed advertisements fill the pages of newspapers and magazines. Poster ads appear in buses, subways, trains, on city walls, etc. Neon signs along downtown streets flash their consumerist messages throughout the night. Billboards dot the roadsides. Commercials interrupt TV and radio programs constantly. No wonder, then, that brand names, logos, trade-

marks, jingles, and slogans have become part and parcel of the
"mental encyclopedia" of virtually everyone who lives in a modern-
day society. Having proven its efficacy in the marketing of economic
goods and services, since the early 1960s advertising has even been
directed with increasing regularity towards matters of social concern.
Anti-smoking and anti-drug campaigns are examples of the use of
advertising techniques as means to promote public welfare. And,
needless to say, the use of advertising in the political arena seems to
know no bounds. Politicians at all levels of government now communicate their platforms during political campaigns and their personal perspectives on social issues regularly through sleek persuasive
forms of advertising.

Contemporary advertising is characterizable as a blend of *art*
and *science*, because it employs both aesthetic techniques designed
to influence how people perceive goods and services, and the tools of
psychology and statistics to assess the effects of such techniques on
consumer behavior. Advertisers and marketing agencies conduct extensive surveys to determine the potential acceptance of brand
names, logos, etc. before they are advertised at costs that may add up
to millions of dollars. If the survey convinces the manufacturer that
several versions of, say, a package design, a logo, or a brand name,
will appeal to a small number of purchasers, a research crew will
then determine the extent to which a larger sample of consumers will
react to them. After the one or two best-liked versions are identified,
the advertiser produces a limited quantity of products with the new
package design, or bearing the new brand name or logo, and then introduces them in a test market. The results of this final procedure
will tell the advertiser which version is the most appealing one.

Advertising is also used commonly in *propaganda*, *publicity*, and
public relations. *Propaganda* is the craft of spreading and entrenching doctrines, views, beliefs, etc. reflecting specific interests and ide-
ologies (political, social, philosophical, etc.) by attempting to persuade people through rational or emotional appeals. *Publicity* is the
art of disseminating any information that concerns a person, group,
event, or product through some public medium so as to garner attention for the individual, group, etc. *Public relations* is the profession
employing activities and techniques designed to establish favorable

attitudes and responses towards organizations, institutions, and/or individuals.

Advertising can thus be seen to fall into three main categories:

(1) *consumer advertising*, which is directed towards the promotion of some product or service to the general public (or market segment thereof) through all types of media (print, electronic, etc.);

(2) *trade advertising*, which is directed to dealers and professionals through appropriate trade publications and media;

(3) *public relations advertising* (including advertising for reasons of propaganda and/or publicity), which is directed towards society by citizens or community groups, or by politicians, corporations, etc., in order to promote some issue of social concern or a political agenda, to enhance the popularity of some person (e.g. a political candidate), etc.

The focus of this book is on the first type, which can be defined more specifically for our purposes as the craft of deploying any appropriate *representational strategy* that will demonstrably enhance the salability of a marketable good and/or service. Already at the turn of the twentieth century, the increasing success of consumer advertising in enhancing the salability of goods and services gave birth in 1914 to the *Audit Bureau of Circulations* in the United States, an independent organization founded and supported by newspaper and magazine publishers wishing to obtain circulation statistics and to standardize the ways of presenting them. Then, in 1936, the *Advertising Research Foundation* was established to conduct research on, and to develop, advertising techniques with the capacity to boost the authenticity, reliability, efficiency, and usefulness of all advertising and marketing research. Today, the increasing sophistication with statistical information-gathering and data-processing techniques makes it possible for advertisers to direct their advertising campaigns to specific "market segments," i.e. populations of people classified on the basis of where they live, what income they make, what educational background they have, etc. in order to determine their susceptibility to, or inclination towards, certain products.

The purpose of this chapter is to present an overview of the *art* and *science* of advertising. We will start with a schematic history of the field, focusing on the factors that have entrenched advertising's forms of representation into social discourse. Then, we will describe how these forms are designed to persuade consumers to acquire specific goods and/or services. Lastly, we will introduce the science of semiotics as the discipline that is highly suited to the analysis of advertising, discussing the main semiotic axioms and notions that can be used in this field of application.

1.1 A schematic history of advertising

Most historians believe that outdoor signs displayed above the shop doors of several ancient cities of the Middle East were the first advertising artifacts of human civilization. As early as 3000 BC, the Babylonians, who lived in what is now Iraq, used such signs to advertise the stores themselves. The ancient Greeks and Romans also hung signs outside their shops. Since few people could read, the merchants of the era used recognizable visual symbols carved in stone, clay, or wood for their signs. In ancient Egypt, merchants hired *criers* to walk through the streets announcing the arrivals of ships and their cargo.

A poster found in Thebes in 1000 BC is now considered to be one of the world's first print ads. In large letters, it offered a whole gold coin for the capture of a runaway slave. Archeologists have found similar kinds of posters scattered all over ancient societies. An outdoor poster found among the ruins of ancient Rome, for instance, offers property for rent; an announcement found painted on a wall in Pompeii calls the attention of travelers to a tavern located in a different town; and the list of such relics could go on and on. Throughout history, poster and picture advertising in marketplaces and temples have, in fact, constituted popular means of disseminating information and of promoting the barter and sale of goods and services.

The use of shop signs, posters, and town *criers* continued uninterrupted right into medieval times, to the great advantage of the merchants of that era. But it was the invention of the modern printing press by Johann Gutenberg (c. 1400-1468) in the fifteenth century that transformed advertising into a craft of persuasion, since Gutenberg's invention made the printed word available to masses of people. Fliers and posters could be printed quickly and cheaply, and posted in public places or inserted in books, pamphlets, newspapers, etc. The printing press also spawned a new form of advertising known as the *handbill*. This had an advantage over a poster or sign because it could be reproduced and distributed to many people living near and far apart.

Up until the early part of the seventeenth century, advertising texts (posters, signs, handbills, etc.) were created as independent artifacts, i.e. as texts in their own right, to promote specific goods, services, etc. But, by the latter part of the century, when newspapers were beginning to circulate widely, print advertising was being used, more and more, in tandem with publications designed for other purposes. Advertising was fast becoming, clearly, an intrinsic part of the "Gutenberg Galaxy," as the Canadian communications theorist Marshall McLuhan (1911-1980) characterized the radical new social order that ensued from the utilization of print technology. According to McLuhan (1962), the advent of print technology ushered in the process of globalizing ideas and of inducing the widespread feeling that knowledge and truth existed in some *objective* form. Print introduces a level of abstraction that forces people to separate the maker of knowledge from the knowledge made. And this in turn leads to the perception that knowledge can exist on its own, spanning time and distance. Before printed knowledge became widespread, humans lived primarily in oral cultures, based on the spoken word. The human voice cannot help but convey emotion, overtly or implicitly. So, the kind of consciousness that develops in people living in oral cultures is shaped by the emotionality of the voice. In such cultures, the knower and the thing known are seen typically as inseparable. On the other hand, in print cultures, the kind of consciousness that develops is shaped by the written page, with its edges, margins, and sharply defined characters organized in neatly-layered rows or columns, inducing a linear-rational way of thinking in people. In such cultures, the knowledge encoded in writing is perceived as separable from the encoder of that knowledge primarily because the maker of the written text is not present during the reading and understanding of the text. In the Gutenberg Galaxy advertising texts thus came to be viewed as *rational* statements about the *objective* qualities of products, independently of the makers of these products and of their pecuniary motives.

The *London Gazette* became the first newspaper to reserve a section exclusively for advertising. So successful was this venture that by the end of the seventeenth century several agencies came into existence for the specific purpose of creating newspaper ads for merchants and artisans. In general, they designed the texts in the style of modern classifieds, without illustrative support. But the ads nonetheless had all the persuasive rhetorical flavor of their contemporary descendants. The ad makers of the era catered to the wealthy clients who bought and read newspapers, promoting the sale of tea, coffee, wigs, books, theater tickets, and the like. The following advertisement for toothpaste dates back to a 1660 ad published in the *Gazette*. What is captivating about it is the fact that its rhetorical style is virtually identical to the one used today for the promotion of this type of product (cited by Dyer 1982: 16-17):

> Most excellent and proved Dentifrice to scour and cleanse the Teeth, making them white as ivory, preserves the Tooth-ach; so that being constantly used, the Parties using it are never troubled with the Tooth-ach. It fastens the Teeth, sweetens the Breath, and preserves the Gums and Mouth from cankers and Impothumes, and the right are only to be had at Thomas Rookes, Stationer.

The earliest newspaper ads in the United States were classified ads published in 1704 in the Boston *News-Letter*. Print advertising spread rapidly throughout the eighteenth century in both Europe and America, proliferating to the point that the writer and lexicographer Samuel Johnson (1709-1784) felt impelled to make the following statement in *The Idler*: "Advertisements are now so numerous that they are very negligently perused, and it is therefore become necessary to gain attention by magnificence of promise and by eloquence sometimes sublime and sometimes pathetic" (cited by Panati 1984: 168).

As print advertising started becoming a fixture of the social landscape in the pre-industrialized world, ad creators began paying more attention to the design and layout of the ad text. With the advent of industrialization in the nineteenth century, *style of presentation* became increasingly important in raising the persuasive efficacy of the ad text. The syntactically cumbersome and visually-uninteresting ads of the previous century were replaced more and more by layouts using words set out in blocks, compact sentences, and contrasting type fonts. New language forms were coined regularly to fit the needs of the manufacturer. As a consequence, advertising was surreptitiously starting to change the very structure and use of language and verbal communication, as more and more people became exposed to advertising in newspapers, magazines, on posters, and the like. Everything from clothes to beverages was being promoted through ingenious new techniques which included:

- strategic repetitions of the firm's name or of the product in the composition of the ad text;

- the use of compact phrases set in eye-catching patterns (vertically, horizontally, diagonally);

- the use of contrasting font styles and formats, along with supporting illustrations;

- the creation of slogans and neologisms designed to highlight some quality of the product.

As the nineteenth century came to a close, American advertisers in particular were, as Dyer (1982: 32) aptly points out, using "more colloquial, personal and informal language to address the customer" and also exploiting certain effective rhetorical devices including "the uses of humour to attract attention to a product." So persuasive had this new form of advertising become that, by the early decades of the twentieth century, it started becoming a component of social discourse, starting to change some of the basic ways in which people communicated with each other and in which they perceived commodities and services.

1.1.1 The modern era

The growing use and influence of advertising in the nineteenth century led to the establishment of the first advertising agency by Philadelphia entrepreneur Volney B. Palmer in 1842. By 1849, Palmer had offices in New York, Boston, and Baltimore in addition to his Philadelphia office. In 1865, George P. Rowell began contracting with local newspapers as a go-between with clients. Ten years later, in 1875, N. W. Ayer and Son, another Philadelphia advertising agency, became a rival of Rowell and Palmer. In time, the firm hired writers and artists to create print ads and carried out complete advertising campaigns for clients. It thus became the first *ad agency* in the modern sense of the word. By 1900, most agencies in the United States were writing ads for clients, and were starting to assume responsibility for complete advertising campaigns. By the 1920s, such agencies had become themselves large business enterprises, constantly developing new techniques and methods that would be capable of influencing the *typical consumer*. The following advice, given by one of the early advertising agents - a man named Claude Hopkins - to prospective ad copywriters in the early part of the century, is illustrative of the mindset that was starting to take shape in the business of advertising at large (quoted by Bendinger 1988: 14):

> Don't think of people in the mass. That gives you a blurred view. Think of a typical individual, man or woman, who is likely to want what you sell. The advertising man studies the consumer. He tries to place himself in the position of the buyer. His success largely depends on doing that to the exclusion of everything else.

Between 1890 and 1920 industrial corporations grew into mammoth structures that transformed the workplace into an integrated economic system of mass production. It was at that point in time that advertising came to be perceived primarily as an instrument of persuasion by corporate executives. Business and psychology had joined forces by the first decades of the twentieth century. From the 1920s onwards, advertising agencies sprang up all over, broadening the attempts of their predecessors to build a rhetorical bridge between the product and the consumer's consciousness. Everything from product name, design, and packaging came gradually within the purview of the advertising business.

In the 1920s, the increased use of electricity led to the possibility of further entrenching advertising into the social landscape through the use of new electronic media. Electricity made possible the illuminated outdoor poster; and photoengraving and other printing inventions helped both the editorial and advertising departments of magazines create truly effective illustrative material that could be incorporated into ad texts. The advent of radio, also in the 1920s, led to the invention and widespread use of a new form of advertising, known as the *commercial* - a mini-narrative or musical jingle revolving around a product or service and its uses. The commercial became immediately a highly persuasive form of advertising, since it could reach masses of potential customers, print literate or not, instantaneously. The commercial became even more influential as a vehicle for disseminating advertising messages throughout society with the advent of television in the late 1940s. TV commercials of the day, such as *Folger's* coffee's pseudoscientific sales pitches, *Mum* deodorant's satires of spy movies, and *Pepsodent* toothpaste's animations with snappy jingles, became so familiar that perception of the product became inextricably intertwined with the style and content of the commercials created to promote it. The commercial also created the first advertising personalities, from *Mr. Clean* (representing a detergent product of the same name) to *Speedy* (a personified *Alka-Seltzer* tablet); and it became a source of dissemination of recognizable tunes throughout society, from *Mr. Clean in a just a minute* (for the *Mr. Clean* detergent product) to *Plop, plop, fizz, fizz oh what a relief it is* (for the *Alka-Seltzer* stomach product).

Recently, the Internet has come forward to complement and supplement both the *print* and *commercial* (radio and TV) forms of advertising. Even though Internet users can search through sources ranging from vast databases to small electronic "bulletin boards," advertising textuality has not changed drastically from the way it has been fashioned by the medium of Television. Like TV, the Internet uses graphics, audio, and various visual techniques to enhance the effectiveness of its ad texts.

It should also be mentioned that, ever since Vance Packard's 1957 indictment of advertising as a surreptitious form of persuasion, in his widely read work *The Hidden Persuaders*, the entire enterprise has come constantly under attack in the United States, although no consensus has yet been reached as to its effects on the ethos and mores of people living in consumerist cultures. Ironically, advertising is used regularly by both "right-wing" groups, who attack it for promoting secular humanism and promiscuity, and by "left-wing" ones, who attack it instead for deceitfully influencing and promoting stereotypical role models and unabashed consumerism. All this "proves," paradoxically, that advertising has indeed become an intrinsic component of modern-day social discourse. The language of advertising has become the language of all - even of those who are critical of it. As Twitchell (2000: 1) aptly puts it, "language about products and services has pretty much replaced language about all other subjects." It is no exaggeration to claim that today most of our information, intellectual stimulation, and lifestyle models come from, or are related to, advertising images. We assimilate and react to advertising texts unwittingly, and, in ways that parallel how individuals and groups have responded in the past to religious texts, we utilize such texts unconsciously as templates for planning, interpreting, and structuring social actions and behaviors. Advertising has become one of the most ubiquitous, all-encompassing forms of social discourse ever devised by humans - it is estimated that the average American is exposed to over 3000 advertisements a day and watches three years' worth of television commercials over the course of a lifetime (Kilbourne 1999). As McLuhan quipped, the *medium* in this case has indeed become the *message*.

At this point, it is useful to adopt the historical framework devised by Leiss, Kline and Jhally (1990: 5), which we have modified slightly here, so as to summarize the main themes that were implicit in the foregoing historical sketch. The term *rational* refers to the *objectiveness* quality that print advertising generates (1.1). This implies that the ad text is designed to appeal primarily to the consumer's rational mind, and that the focus of the ad message is on the utility of the product, on its qualities, on its price, etc. The term *non-rational* refers instead to the more *emotional* quality associated with electronic advertising (radio, television, Internet). This implies that the focus of advertising is on promoting product personality or on the lifestyle aspects related to the utilization of the product (table 1):

Table 1.   Summary of the main trends in advertising

	Media		
	Print	**Radio**	**Television/Internet**
Strategy	rational	non-rational	non-rational
Period	Middle Ages-1920	1920-1950	1950-present
Focus	product qualities, price, use, etc.	personality attributes associated with product	types of lifestyle activities associated with product
Themes	quality, usefulness, etc.	status, family, health, social authority, etc.	glamour, romance, sensuality, self-transformation, leisure, health, groups, friendship, etc.

The *rational* vs. *non-rational* dichotomy is quickly disappearing from contemporary advertising, as all forms of advertising, including the print ones, are becoming less and less designed to appeal to the reasoning mind (rational) and more and more to the emotions (non-rational). Since the 1920s, in fact, advertising has emphasized the emotional attributes associated with a product - status, family, etc. - and on creating a "personality" for the product. It has become, as mentioned above, a *representational art*.

1.1.2 Positioning and image-creation

The two main techniques that characterize the ways in which non-rational advertising goes about creating its messages and anchoring them firmly into social discourse are called *positioning* and *image-creation*. *Positioning* is the placing or targeting of a product for the right people. For example, ads for *Budweiser* beer are normally positioned for a male audience, whereas ads for *Chanel* perfume are positioned, by and large, for a female audience. The advertising of the *Mercedes Benz* automobile is aimed at socially upscale car buyers; the advertising of *Dodge* vans is aimed, instead, at middle-class suburban dwellers.

Creating an *image* for a product is fashioning a "personality" for it with which a particular type of consumer can identify. This implies that a product's name, packaging, logo, price, and overall presentation should be contrived in such a way as to create a recognizable *character* for it that is meant to appeal to specific consumer types. Take beer as an example. What kinds of people drink *Budweiser*? And what kinds drink *Heineken* instead? Answers to these questions would typically include remarks about the educational level, class, social attitudes, etc. of the consumer. The one who drinks *Budweiser* is perceived by people as vastly different from the one who drinks *Heineken*. The former is perceived to be a down-to-earth (male) character who simply wants to "hang out with the guys;" the latter a smooth, sophisticated, type (male or female) who appreciates the "finer things" of life. This *personalization* of the product is reinforced further by the fact that *Budweiser* commercials are positioned next to sports events on television, whereas *Heineken* ads are found primarily in lifestyle magazines. The idea behind creating an *image* for the product is, clearly, to speak directly to particular *types* of individuals, not to everyone, so that these individuals can see their own personalities represented in the lifestyle images created by advertisements for certain products.

The image associated with certain kinds of products is further entrenched by an advertising technique that can be called *mythologization*. This is the strategy of imbuing brand names, logos, product design, ads, and commercials intentionally with some mythic meaning. For instance, the quest for beauty, the conquest of death, among other mythic themes, are constantly being woven into the specific textualities that advertisers create for certain products. In the case of beauty products, this strategy often can be literally seen in the personages that populate ads and commercials. These are, typically, charming beautiful people, with a deified quality about the way they look.

Another way in which advertisers entrench product *image* effectively is through *logo* design. Take as an example the *McDonald's* golden arches logo. Most people today go to fast-food restaurants to be with family or with friends, so as to get a meal quickly, and/or because the atmosphere is congenial. Most people would also admit that the food at a *McDonald's* restaurant is affordable and that the service is fast and polite. Indeed, many people today probably feel more "at home" at a *McDonald's* restaurant than in their own households. This is, in fact, the semiotic key to unlocking the meaning that the *McDonald's* logo is designed to create. The arches reverberate with mythic symbolism, beckoning good people to march through them triumphantly into a paradise of law and order, cleanliness, friendliness, hospitality, hard work, self-discipline, and family values. In a sense, *McDonald's* is comparable to an organized religion. From the menu to the uniforms, *McDonald's* exacts and imposes standardization, in the same way that the world's organized religions impose standardized interpretations of their sacred texts and uniformity in the appearance and behavior of their clergy. The message created unconsciously by the golden arches logo is therefore that, like paradise, *McDonald's* is a place that will "do it all for you," as one of the company's slogans so aptly phrases it.

All this shows the power of advertising to influence collective perceptions. A fast food eatery would be inconceivable in a non-consumerist culture, and would have been unimaginable even in a consumerist one not so long ago. The popularity of *McDonald's* and other fast-food restaurants is, as advertisers obviously know, tied to the socioeconomic need for a two-income household. Fewer and fewer modern-day families have the time to eat meals together within the household, let alone the energy to prepare elaborate dinners. And even when they do, it is highly unlikely that they will perceive the eating event as a structured one aimed at preserving family harmony and traditional moral values. In modern-day households, meals are routinely consumed in front of television sets. The home, ironically, has become a place where people now tend to eat apart. Enter *McDonald's*, to the rescue, as the advertisers proclaim! Eating at *McDonald's* is affordable, quick, and cheery; it is a place where the family can eat together, at the same table, with no TV or other distraction. All these socioeconomic meanings are embedded in the symbolism that is built into the advertising of the *McDonald's* product, from the *logo* to the *Ronald McDonald* figure and the jingles and slogans that beckon people to pass through the golden arches.

1.1.3 The era of persuasion

Since the end of the nineteenth century, advertising has succeeded, more so than any economic process or socio-political movement, in promoting and ensconcing consumerism as a way of life. By proposing marketplace solutions to virtually all social problems, it has become a form of persuasive discourse that has become an end itself. No wonder, then, that the shopping malls are filled with thrill-seekers who would otherwise become stir crazy. Perhaps, as many social critics warn, we do indeed live in a world conjured up by lifestyle ads and TV commercials. Stuart Ewen (1988: 20) puts it eloquently in the following manner:

> If the "life-style" of style is not realizable in life, it is nevertheless the most constantly available lexicon from which many of us draw the visual grammar of our lives. It is a behavioral model that is closely interwoven with modern patterns of survival and desire. It is a hard to define but easy to recognize element in our current history.

The emergence of our "ad-mediated world," as some critics now characterize modern civilization, occurred, as we saw above, in the decades between 1890 and 1920 when industrial corporations adopted advertising, not just as a means for informing people about the availability and qualities of their goods and services, but primarily for associating lifestyle choices with the acquisition of specific products. Business and the *psychology of persuasion* had obviously joined forces by the first decades of the twentieth century. Since the 1920s, positioning and image-creation have become the primary techniques of what has come to be known as the *era of persuasion* in advertising. This is an era in which advertising messages have moved away from describing the product in itself to focusing on the consumer of the product, creating product imagery with which the consumer can easily identify (Woodward and Denton 1988: 192). Advertisers are now creating brand names, logos, package designs, bottle shapes, print ads, and electronic commercials that, below their literal appearance, tap into unconscious desires, urges, and mythic motifs embedded in the human psyche. Certainly, as we shall see in the remainder of this book, the technique of mythologization has become part and parcel of image-creation for most, if not all, lifestyle products (perfumes, colognes, shoes, etc.). And for the other kinds of products and services, ads and commercials now offer the same kinds of promise and hope to which religions and social philosophies once held exclusive rights - security against the hazards of old age, better positions in life, popularity and personal prestige, social advancement, better health, happiness, etc. In a phrase, the modern advertiser stresses not the product, but the benefits that may be expected to ensue from its purchase. And, as we shall see in this book, the advertiser is becoming more and more adept at setting foot into the same subconscious regions of psychic experience that were once explored only by philosophers, artists, and religious thinkers.

1.1.4 The entrenchment of advertising in social discourse

To conclude this schematic journey through the history of advertising, it should be emphasized one more time that, because of the growing effectiveness of its persuasion techniques, advertising has become entrenched into social discourse by virtue of its widespread diffusion throughout society. Everywhere one turns, one is bound to find some ad message designed to persuade people to buy a product, to endorse a political candidate, to support a cause, and so on and so forth. Business firms, political parties and candidates, social organizations, special-interest groups, and governments alike advertise routinely to create favorable "images" of themselves in the minds of people. As mentioned several times, all this leads to the inescapable conclusion that advertising has developed, since the first decades of the twentieth century, into a privileged form of *social discourse* that has unparalleled rhetorical force. The categories of this discourse are, however, highly ephemeral and vacuous. This is, of course, intentional. The inbuilt ephemerality of advertising language and style of visual presentation makes it possible to:

- guarantee that newness and faddishness can be reflected in the product through adaptive change in the style and content of ads and commercials, or in the meanings embedded into its logo, package design, etc.;

- ensure that any changes in social trends (fashion, music, social values, popularity of media personalities, etc.) also be reflected in ads, commercials, logos, design, etc.;

- ensure that the product's identity keep in step with the times by renaming it, redesigning its appearance, changing its advertising textuality, etc.;

- guarantee that the consumer's changing needs and perceptions be built into the textuality (form and content) of brand names, logos, package designs, ads, and commercials, thus creating a dynamic interplay between advertising and changing modalities of social lifestyle, whereby one influences the other through a constant synergy.

We refer to advertising as a form of *discourse* in the sense that it has influenced not only the structure of language and the modality of lifestyle, but also the content of routine daily acts of communicative exchanges. Many meanings in common interactions between people can be understood only if knowledge (at least in part) of a specific ad campaign or style of promotion is known. Few people would recognize today that a simple expression such as *Join the new generation* has become widespread because of *Pepsi's* highly successful *Join the Pepsi Generation* campaign of a few years back. Social communication is a highly adaptive and context-sensitive mode of interaction that is shaped by forces that are largely external to it. The rules of this form of communication are highly susceptible to the subtle influences that the cultural situation in which people live has on them. As the great Estonian semiotician Yuri Lotman (1922-1993) pointed out, human communication is governed by a cultural *textuality* that makes it itself noticeable in dialoguing exchanges between people. This textuality bestows a sense of wholeness and unity upon routine communication. Lotman (1990: 138) puts it perceptively as follows: "The entire space of the semiosphere is transected by boundaries of different levels," which in turn create "a multileveled system."

The point of the foregoing discussion has been to emphasize that these *boundaries* are being established, more and more, by the categories of advertising textuality, which now mediate between all kinds of messages and how we perceive them. Since advertising textuality is instant and highly variegated, it should come as little surprise to find that people exposed to large doses of it on a daily basis tend to develop short attention spans and require constant variety in the information they take in. We have, in effect, become habituated to such large doses of information and to the many catchy phrases edited and stylized for effortless mass consumption.

The ultimate goal of creating an appropriate image for a product is to embed it into social consciousness. But the advertising industry does not stop there. It attempts to further embed product recognizability into such consciousness by a host of complementary ploys. Following are the most common ones:

* the something-for-nothing lure (*Buy one and get a second one free! Send for free sample! Trial offer at half price! No money down!* etc.);

* the use of humor to generate a feeling of pleasantness towards a product;

* endorsement by celebrities to make a product appear reliable;

- inducing parents to believe that giving their children certain products will secure them a better life and future;

- appealing to children to "ask mummy or daddy" to buy certain products, thus increasing the likelihood that parents will "give in" to their children's requests;

- using *scare copy* techniques designed to promote such goods and services as insurance, fire alarms, cosmetics, and vitamin capsules by evoking the fear of poverty, sickness, loss of social standing, and/or impending disaster;

- creating brand names, logos, packaging designs, magazine ads and radio and television commercials that are highly suggestive of erotic, sensual, mythic, and other kinds of psychologically powerful themes.

These techniques have become so intrinsic to the practice of advertising that they are no longer recognized consciously as stratagems. Advertising has become the fuel for an entertainment-driven society that seeks artifice as part of its routine of escapism from the deeper philosophical questions that would otherwise beset it.

Humor has become particularly fundamental in advertising, showing an understanding on the part of ad-makers of the highly satirical, ironic mindset of today's signifying orders. Typically, the humor used is consistent with that used on TV and cinema, and reflected in society at large. In this way, it can be used in line with what makes people laugh, thus making the product or service appear contemporary and friendly.

Advertising is powerful because it offers recognizable "objects," "solutions," "advice," etc. that promise the hope of more money and better jobs, security against the hazards of old age and illness, popularity and personal prestige, praise from others, more comfort, increased enjoyment or pleasure, social advancement, improved appearance, better health, erotic stimulation, popularity, emotional security, and so on. The effectiveness of the techniques used to engender product recognizability is limited only by the ingenuity of the advertiser, by the limits of the various channels of communications used to disseminate product recognizability, by certain legal restrictions in place where the advertising messages are delivered, and by standards self-imposed by the advertising industry.

1.2 The semiotic approach to advertising

Given the obvious influence that advertising has had on the development of modern cultures, the French semiotician Roland Barthes (1915-1980) drew attention in the 1950s to the value of studying its messages and techniques with the theoretical tools of the science of *semiotics*. After the publication of his pivotal book *Mythologies* in 1957, a new branch of research in semiotics in fact sprang up, focusing on how advertising generates its meanings, animating, at the same time, a society-wide debate on the broader ethical and cultural questions raised by the entrenchment of advertising as a form of discourse in contemporary societies. Particularly worrisome to Barthes was the fact that the constant change in advertising styles, techniques, and modes of delivery tended to create an incessant craving for new goods. He called this culturally induced state of mind *neomania*, which he defined simply as an obsessive desire for new objects of consumption. Barthes also scathingly criticized the use of mythologizing techniques which, he claimed, elevated shopping to much more than just acquiring the essentials required for daily living; it bestowed upon it the same kinds of meanings that come from religious experiences.

A recent example of the plausibility of the Barthesian thesis is the *Absolut Vodka* campaign of the 1980s and 1990s which, as O'Neill-Karch (2000: 11-12) has clearly shown, went so far as to imbue its product with the spiritual qualities that are perceived to be so lacking in the hubris of modern secular societies. It started with a bottle shown with a halo and the caption *Absolut Perfection*; it then progressed to a winged bottle with the caption *Absolut Heaven*; and, after that, to a bottle held by the hand of a medieval knight with the caption *Absolut Grail* (in medieval legend the grail was the plate or cup from which Christ drank at the Last Supper and which Joseph of Arimathea used to receive the blood from the wounds of the crucified Christ). The overall message of the campaign was rather transparent - spirituality could be obtained by imbibing the vodka.

Barthes inspired the first true semiotic works analyzing the implicit messages of advertising. Today, the semiotic investigation of advertising and marketing has become widespread and has produced some truly interesting studies (e.g. Seiter 1987; Umiker-Sebeok 1987; Umiker-Sebeok, Cossette and Bachand 1988; Umiker-Sebeok 1989; Alexander, Burt, and Collinson 1995; Harris 1995; Goldman and Papson 1996; Berger 1996, 2000; Warren 1997; Todenhagen 1999; Beasley, Danesi, and Perron 2000). If there is one theme that stands out from this line of inquiry, which is of specific relevance to the subject matter of this textbook, it is that many brand names, logos, package designs, ads, and commercials are interpretable at two levels - a "surface" level and an "underlying" one. The former involves the use of specific types of signs in a highly creative manner to create a personality for the product (images, words, colors, repeating stories, etc.). These are both "reflexes" of, and "traces" to, the underlying level - where the concealed meaning of the text lies: i.e. the surface elements cohere into a *textuality* that conjures up an array of meanings embedded in the underlying level. More often than not, these are mythic, or archetypal, meanings, as Barthes argued in many of his writings on the media and popculture, and thus work psychologically at a subthreshold level of mind. This is why ads for lifestyle products often utilize genital and/or taboo ritualistic symbols in the surface level, which are typically beyond the threshold of direct awareness. This embedding of connotative meanings in the underlying level circumvents the inevitable criticism that people would invariably direct at advertisers. Indeed, when the underlying subtext is decoded people tend to become alarmed and repulsed by the "hidden" message.

1.2.1 Signification systems

The goal of semiotics in the study of advertising is, ultimately, to unmask the arrays of hidden meanings in the underlying level, which form what can be called *signification systems*. As is well known, modern-day semiotic method is based on the writings of the American logician Charles S. Peirce (1839-1914) and the French linguist Ferdinand de Saussure (1857-1913). For the sake of historical accuracy, it should be mentioned that semiotics grew out of the study by the ancient physicians of the Western world of the physiological symptoms produced by particular diseases. The term *semiotics* (spelled originally *semeiotics*), from Greek *semeion* "mark, sign," was coined by the founder of Western medical science, Hippocrates (460-377 BC). A *symptom* is, in fact, a perfect example of what a *semeion* is. It is a noticeable sign - a dark bruise, a rash, a sore throat, etc. - that stands for some physical condition - a broken finger, a skin allergy, a cold, etc. Symptomatology was further developed by Galen (129-199? AD), the most outstanding physician of antiquity after Hippocrates.

Medical science is, in effect, basic semiotic science, since it is grounded on the principle that the symptom is a trace to an inner state, condition, etc. The fundamental thing to notice about the *semeion* is that it is interpretable in terms of two dimensions, namely the discernible symptom itself (with all its physical characteristics) and the probable condition it indicates (with all its predictable consequences). The two are inseparable: i.e. there is no symptom that is not caused by some bodily condition, and, vice versa, there is no condition that does not produce symptoms (detectable or not by human observation).

The *semeion* is a *natural sign*, i.e. a sign produced by Nature. But humans have also produced their own signs - e.g. words, gestures, symbols, etc. - that can stand for things other than bodily conditions or the things of Nature (flora, fauns, etc.). These are called *conventional signs*, since they are invented by human beings in cultural settings for conventionalized purposes. Like natural signs, they also consist of two dimensions:

(1) a physical dimension: e.g. the sounds or letters that make up a word such as *cat*; the configuration made by the fingers in hand gesturing, etc.

(2) the entity, object, being, event, etc. that the physical part has been created to stand for, whether it be real or imagined.

The physical dimension (1) is called the *signifier* in Saussurean semiotics and *representamen* in Peircean semiotics; the conceptual dimension (2) is called *signified* and *object* in the two methods respectively. In this book we will use Saussurean terminology both for the sake of convenience, and because it was primarily Saussurean semioticians, like Roland Barthes, who wrote about advertising from the perspective of sign theory. The particular kinds of meanings that the association of a *signifier* with a *signified* (or set of signifieds) generates in social situations is called *signification*.

Conventional signs are classified as *verbal* and *nonverbal*; words and other linguistic structures (expressions, phrases, etc.) are examples of *verbal signs*; drawings, gestures, etc. are examples of *nonverbal signs*. Conventional signs serve a fundamental need in human cognitive life. They allow humans to remember the world. Knowing and using words and figures permit people to recognize the same things over and over in all kinds of situations. Without signs we would have to experience things and represent them anew each time we came across them or each time we imagined them. Signs are found in all forms of representation and communication. They make thinking and communication fluid and routine.

The diagnosis of the "meaning" of a sore throat can be used to show how semioticians (not to mention doctors) go about conducting their investigations. First, the semiotician/doctor would see it instantly as a *semeion*, because it is something physically discernible standing for something other than itself. The particular term used to designate the physical part of the *semeion* itself - which in this case is characterizable as an observable "redness" producing an appreciable soreness - is the signifier. Next, the semiotician/doctor would consider the *context* or location of the redness (in this case the throat). This determines, or at least constrains, the potential condition that it identifies - soreness in other parts of the body would, in fact, indicate different medical conditions. This is the signified. Through previous experience, doctors can safely predict, in most cases, that sore throats are caused by such conditions as colds, infections, etc.

This is called the *signification system* to which the semeion is ascribed. The term *interpretation* is sometimes used instead of *signification* - although this has many other meanings in semiotics.

A *signification system* in advertising can thus be defined as the set of meanings that are generated for a product by a systematic association of various signifiers (brand name, logo, ad texts, etc.) with implicit signifieds relating to personality, lifestyle, desires, etc. Take, as a simple example, the name *Acura* given to a Japanese automobile. The obvious suggestion of *accuracy* in automobile design and performance is self-evident in this name. It is also imitative of Japanese word structure, as can be seen in a word such as *tempura*. This reinforces the connection to Japanese culture and the widely-held view that Japan is at the cutting edge of technology. But, in addition, the signifier has been constructed at the same time to be imitative of the structure of an Italian word. The *-a* ending of the word would indicate the feminine gender in Italian grammar and thus, by metaphorical extension, femininity (Danesi 1998). Now, this simple feature of the signifier, *Acura*, generates a system of connotations that are based on perceived qualities ascribed traditionally to the Italian language and its speakers. The great romantic English poet, Lord Byron (1788–1824), described Italian as a language that sounds "as if it should be writ on satin." Byron's description is not an isolated expression of poetic fancy, but, in actual fact, a popular view of the Italian language across the world, often called the language of "love," "poetry," and "song." It is also a popular view that Italians are "artistic," "romantic," "friendly," and so on.

This array of meanings constitutes the *signification system* built into the name *Acura* (figure 1):

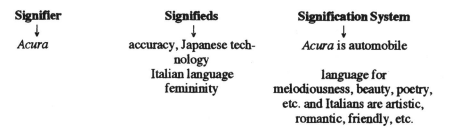

Signifier	Signifieds	Signification System
↓	↓	↓
Acura	accuracy, Japanese technology	*Acura* is automobile
	Italian language	language for
	femininity	melodiousness, beauty, poetry, etc. and Italians are artistic, romantic, friendly, etc.

Figure 1. Signification system generated by the brand name *Acura*

The thing to notice about this, and all signification systems, is that it is open-ended. As we shall see in the third chapter (3.2.1), such systems are characterizable as endless *connotative chains*. It is, in fact, a connotative chain that is embedded in the image of the *Acura* automobile:

> *Acura = Japanese technology = accuracy = Italian = melodiousness = beauty = poetry = artistic = romantic = friendly = etc.*

This analysis, in microcosm, constitutes the essence of the semiotic study advertising. In effect, semiotic analysis consists in fleshing out *signification* relations between *signifiers* and *signifieds* in brand names, logos, package designs, ad texts, and commercials by asking questions such as the following:

- Who or what created the name, logo. ad text, etc.?

- What does it mean in its underlying level?

- How does it deliver this meaning?

- What signifiers (verbal, nonverbal, etc.) were employed?

- What possible signifieds do these allude to?

- What signification system does it generate?

- How many interpretations (signification systems) are possible under the circumstances?

1.2.2 A brief trek through the history of semiotics

Semiotics is to be differentiated from what has come to be known in the last fifty years as *communication science*. Although the two share much of the same conceptual and methodological territory, communication scientists generally focus more on the technical study of how advertising messages are transmitted (vocally, electronically, etc.), whereas semioticians focus their attention more on what some advertising feature means and on how it generates its meaning.

The fact that human-made signs bear their meanings through social and historical *convention* was first pointed out by Aristotle (384-322 BC) and the Stoic philosophers (a Greek school of philosophy, founded by Zeno of Elea around 308 BC). A little later, it was St. Augustine (354-430 AD), the philosopher and religious thinker, who clearly distinguished between the signs found in Nature - the colors of leaves, the shape of plants, the physiology of symptoms, etc. - and those made by humans - words, symbols, figures, etc. St. Augustine also proposed that in every human sign there exists an implicit *interpretive* dimension that constrains its meaning. This was consistent with the so-called *hermeneutic* tradition established earlier by Clement of Alexandria (150?-215? AD), the Greek theologian and early Father of the Church. *Hermeneutics* is the study and interpretation of ancient texts, especially those of a religious or mythical nature. Today, it is considered, by and large, to be a branch of semiotics aiming to study how all kinds of texts - not just sacred ones - generate meaning. The idea is to establish, as far as possible, the meaning that a text entails on the basis of its specific signs, relevant sources, and historical background. Incidentally, for the sake of historical accuracy, it should be mentioned that the Saussurean notions mentioned above are actually traceable to the medieval Scholastic tradition - a philosophical movement that was dominant in the medieval Christian schools and universities of Europe from about the middle of the eleventh century to about the middle of the fifteenth century. Accepting St. Augustine's basic definition of the sign, as "something that stands for something else," the Scholastics called the two parts that make up the sign as the *signans* (= signifier), defined as something perceptible by the senses, and the *signatum* (= signified), defined as the idea, object, event, etc. to which the sign refers.

John Locke (1632-1704), the English philosopher who set out the principles of empiricism, introduced the formal study of signs into philosophy in his *Essay Concerning Human Understanding* (1690), anticipating that it would allow philosophers to understand the interconnection between representation and knowledge. But the task he laid out remained virtually unnoticed until, as mentioned above, the ideas of the Swiss linguist Ferdinand de Saussure and the American philosopher Charles S. Peirce became the basis for circumscribing an autonomous field of inquiry.

In his *Cours de linguistique générale* (1916), a textbook put together after his death by two of his university students, Saussure used the term *semiology* to designate the field he proposed for studying these structures. But while his term is still used somewhat today, the older term *semiotics* is the preferred one. Saussure emphasized that the study of signs should be divided into two branches - the *synchronic* and the *diachronic*. The former refers to the study of signs at a given point in time, normally the present, and the latter to the investigation of how signs change in form and meaning over time. A large part of the increase in the popularity of the field in the late twentieth century was brought about by the popular fictional writings of Umberto Eco (1932-), a leading practitioner of semiotics. The success of his best-selling novels (*The Name of the Rose, Foucault's Pendulum, The Island of the Day Before*) has stimulated considerable curiosity vis-à-vis semiotics in recent years among the public at large. The work of Thomas A. Sebeok (1920-), a distinguished professor of semiotics at Indiana University, has also been instrumental in showing the relevance of semiotics to those working in cognate disciplines. Sebeok has frequently compared semiotics to a spider's web, because it rarely fails to entrap scientists, educators, and humanists into its intricate loom of insights into human representation.

The application of semiotics to advertising started, as mentioned above, in the work of Roland Barthes, who claimed that the advertising is effective because it utilizes mythic themes to construct its messages. He also showed how specific words, images, colors, and the like form the vocabulary of persuasion in advertising. As the great Polish-born English novelist Joseph Conrad (1857–1924) aptly wrote in 1912 (in his *Personal Record*): "He who wants to persuade should put his trust not in the right argument, but in the right word. The power of sound has always been greater than the power of sense." In effect, the semiotics of advertising can be characterized as a study of the *power of sound and sight*.

1.2.3 Case-in-point 1: High heel shoes

More and more, the techniques used by advertisers are designed to speak *indirectly* to the unconscious level of mind where the so-called

Freudian Id - the unconscious part of the psyche actuated by fundamental impulses toward fulfilling instinctual needs - can be aroused
unwittingly. The sense of touch and smell, which are largely down-
played in our culture, are frequently evoked in an ad text through
synesthesia - a blending of sense experiences - so as to induce an unconscious desire for the product by sensory association. As Barthes
emphasized, any one of the unconscious desires that a culture re-
presses systematically can be manipulated and actuated easily by the
persuasive signs that advertisers utilize into motivating forces and
drives. These accumulate in the psyche, creating an incessant need
for change, for new objects of consumption which, as mentioned
above, Barthes (1967) called neomania. Obsolescence is, in fact,
regularly built into a product, so that the same product can be sold
again and again under new guises.

The semiotic study of the persuasive signs used by advertisers,
Barthes argued, had profound implications for understanding modern
cultures. All the glittery imagery of ads and commercials yells out
one promise to all: "Buy this or that and you will not be bored; you
will be happy or cool." The sad truth is that what we call happiness,
Barthes lamented, cannot be bought. We are living in a very unstable
world psychologically, because it puts much more of a premium on
satisfying consumerist urges than it does on the attainment of wisdom. Advertisers rely on a handful of Epicurean themes - happiness,
youthfulness, success, status, luxury, fashion, beauty - to peddle their
products. They also persuade by intimation and innuendo. You can
Join the Pepsi Generation to be a part of the action, wear a *Benetton*
sweater to help unify the world, or save the environment by buying
some recyclable garbage bag!

The premise that guides semiotic analysis is that the signification systems created by advertising are, more often than not, reflective of innate structures in the sensory, emotional, and intellectual
composition of the human body and the human psyche. This would
explain why the forms of expression that advertising creates, and to
which people respond instinctively the world over, are perceived as
being so appealing. The fundamental *law* of modern-day marketing
can, in fact, be rephrased semiotically as follows - the salability of a
product or service correlates with the effectiveness of a name, logo,
design, ad or commercial to link the product representationally with

some desire or need (erotic, social power, attractiveness, family happiness, etc.).

Consider, for instance, the magazine ads used in various countries to promote fashionable high-heel shoes for young women. A semiotic analysis of such ads is guided by a series of leading questions, such as the following three:

- What are the observable signifiers of the ads?
- What are the signifieds that these signifiers suggest?
- What signification systems are generated?

The thousands of ads for expensive high heel shoes that are published in magazines almost weekly are usually constructed through the process of mythologization. Typically, some attractive young woman is portrayed as wearing the shoes. She is shown with an expression that commonly conveys a kind of sensual rapture that purportedly comes from wearing the shoes. Such ads also utilize contrast effectively. For instance, many use white and black colors or shades to emphasize a contrast between innocence and sexuality (maturity). The ads are, in effect, highly suggestive of the mythology associated with feminine sexuality or "coming-of-age." The way in which such ads have been put together is, in a phrase, strongly suggestive of a "sexualization" of the female body.

But semioticians would not stop at this fairly straightforward analysis of such ads. They would, in fact, go one step further. The world of sex has a long-standing tradition of portrayal in Western mythology. In a representational sense, therefore, these ads are the modern-day advertiser's versions of ancient sexual myths. Many evoke the myth of Persephone, the Greek goddess of fertility and queen of the underworld. Persephone was the daughter of Zeus and Demeter. When she was still a beautiful maiden, Pluto seized her and held her captive in his underworld. Though Demeter eventually persuaded the gods to let her daughter return to her, Persephone was required to remain in the underworld for four months because Pluto had tricked her into eating a pomegranate (food of the dead) there.

When Persephone left the earth, the flowers withered and the grain died, but when she returned, life blossomed anew.

But this is not the only myth that advertisers have enlisted to make generate signification systems for high heel shoes. The myth of Orpheus and Eurydice is another one that is often utilized. Often, several myths are suggested by a specific ad. Actually, it is not important that one or the other mythical *interpretation* of an ad is the correct one; what counts is that a mythical interpretation is possible in the first place. In fact, the more interpretations there are, the more likely the effectiveness of the ad (as will be discussed in subsequent chapters). This suggests a corollary to the fundamental *law* of the marketplace - namely, that the effectiveness of advertising varies according to the suggestive meanings it generates; the more suggestive (or ambiguous), the more effective, thus enhancing product salability.

The original purpose of shoes was, no doubt, to protect the feet and to allow people to walk on hurtful and injurious terrain. But high-heel shoes seem to contravene this function. They are uncomfortable and awkward to wear, yet millions of women wear them. Obviously, the semiotic story of high-heel shoes has other parts to it. In effect, they are accouterments in a system of signification that involves sexuality. High heels date back to the late sixteenth-century. The fashion was encouraged by Louis XIV of France, who apparently wore them to increase his modest height. By the mid-nineteenth century, heeled shoes, low-cut, laced or buttoned to the ankle, became the fashion craze for females. In the twentieth century, according to changing fashion trends, women adopted high, spike, or low heels, with thin, platform, or wedge soles, in closed shoes or sandals. The wearing of high heels as a sexual prop has, in fact, become an entrenched signified in Western culture.

High heels force the body to tilt, thus emphasizing the buttocks and breasts: they highlight the female's sexuality. They also accentuate the role of feet in sexuality. As the social historian William Rossi (1976) has written, across many cultures feet are perceived as sexually desirable. Putting on stockings and high heels on feet is everywhere perceived to be a highly erotic act, and this is borne out by the fact that in most sexual portrayals, women are perceived as looking sexier in stockings and high-heel shoes than without them. Even in fairy tales, the "lure of the shoe" undergirds such stories as *Cinderella* and *The Golden Slipper*.

High heels are *fetishes*. The fetish is a sign that evokes devotion to itself. In some cultures, this devotion is a result of the belief that an object has magical or metaphysical attributes. In our culture, the term refers generally to objects or body parts through which sexual fantasies are played out. Common fetishes in Western society are, in fact, feet, shoes, and articles of intimate female apparel. In a fascinating book on fetishism, however, Valerie Steele (1995) points out that we are all fetishists to a large extent, and that the line between the "normal" and the "abnormal" in sexual mores and practices is vague. Fashion designers, for instance, steal regularly from the fetishist's closet, promoting ultra-high heels, corsets, pointy bras, frilly underwear, latex cat suits. The appropriation has been so complete that people wearing such garments and apparel are unaware of their fetishist origins. To a male, high-heel shoes are erotically exciting. In terms of the signification systems that such ads attempt to tap into, the high heels worn by ad models send out powerful and highly charged sexual signals.

1.3 The role of semiotics in the advertising debate

There are several caveats that must be stated clearly from the very outset when dealing with advertising as the primary focus of semiotic analysis. First, the degree to which an ad, a commercial, an ad campaign, or other strategy will induce consumers to buy the manufacturer's product is an open question. In any case, it is certainly not the point of semiotic analysis to determine this. Simply put, any strategy that is effective *representationally* is effective *psychologically* only to the degree to which consumers can identify with its implicit system of signification. Unlike what Barthes believed, in our view it is not the goal of semiotics to criticize advertisers. On the contrary, semioticians should, in theory, approach an ad or commercial like they would a work of literature or art. The same questions that art and literary critics ask about a painting or a novel are the ones that a semiotician should ask about an ad or a commercial. To the semiotician, advertising provides an opportunity to examine how varied aesthetic experiences, classical forms of expression, and modes of representation are realized in a contemporary medium.

It is interesting to note, parenthetically, that advertising is now one of the most strictly regulated industries in North America (and in some other parts of the world). This bears witness, no doubt, to the perception that it has become indeed a potent form of persuasion. As a consequence, advertisers now have to prepare different versions of an advertisement to comply with varying federal, state, and provincial laws. This is an unfortunate consequence of the "awareness-raising" that the many studies on advertising have brought about since the mid-1950s. The real "protection" against persuasive signification systems is in "understanding" them, not in prohibiting or censoring them.

1.3.1 Semiotics as a form of immunization

If semiotics is to play any role in the society-wide debate on advertising, then it is to provide a form of *immunization*, to use a medical metaphor, against the persuasive messages of advertising that bombard people on a daily basis. This is particularly important for the reason that cultural trends and practices - such as advertising - tend to influence people's notions of what is *natural* in human behavior. Semiotics ultimately allows us to filter the implicit meanings and images that swarm and flow through us every day, immunizing us against becoming passive victims of a situation. By understanding the images, the situation is changed, and we become active interpreters of signs.

This in no way implies that there is a "standard" method of semiotic analysis in the field of advertising. On the contrary, disagreement about what something means is not only unavoidable, but also part of the fun of doing semiotics. Differences of opinion fill the pages of the semiotic research journals and lead, as in other sciences, to a furthering of knowledge in the field. The point of this textbook is simply to put on display the techniques of semiotic analysis, not to provide a series of critical interpretations of ads and commercials. In this way, our hope is that people will end up considering critically *on their own* what kinds of messages they receive on a daily basis and, thus, what to do with them.

It should also be mentioned that semiotics is not a branch of advertising or marketing. It is an autonomous science that aims to investigate *semiosis* - the capacity to produce and comprehend signs - and *representation* - the activity of using signs to make messages and meanings. With few exceptions - e.g. *Semiotic Solutions*, a research-based consultancy agency founded in London by Virginia Valentine which assists image-makers, corporate planners, and product makers in the creation of their strategies, and *ABM* founded by one of the authors of the present text (Ron Beasley), to mention but two - advertising agencies have rarely, as far as we can surmise, sought the aid of semioticians in carrying out their creative activities, including ad style, graphic design, copy writing, print and broadcast production, and research to study audience reaction and response.

1.3.2 The partnership with psychology

Psychologists have, of course, been extremely interested in the persuasion techniques used by advertisers. The school of *psychoanalysis* - the clinical approach to human mental pathologies founded by the psychologist Sigmund Freud (1856-1939) - has been particularly active in studying advertising. The main contribution of this field has been, in our view, that it has exposed how the persuasion techniques used by advertisers are directed to the *unconscious* region of the human mind. Psychoanalysts claim that it is this region which contains our hidden wishes, memories, fears, feelings, and images that are prevented from gaining expression by the conscious part of the mind. The brilliant Swiss psychologist Carl Jung (1875-1961) saw Freud's interpretation of the unconscious as too narrow. Jung accepted Freud's basic idea, but he divided the unconscious instead into two regions: a *personal unconscious*, containing the feelings and thoughts developed by an individual that are directive of his/her particular life schemes, and a *collective unconscious*, containing the feelings and thoughts developed cumulatively by the species that are directive of its overall life pattern. Jung described the latter as a "receptacle" of primordial images shared by all humanity that have become such an intrinsic part of the unconscious as to be beyond reflection. So, they gain expression instead in the symbols and forms that constitute the myths, tales, tunes, rituals, and the like that are found in cultures across the world. He called these universal images *archetypes*. For instance, the phallic symbols that advertising incorporates typically into its lifestyle ads appeal instinctively in approximately the same ways in all humans, virtually irrespective of age, because they constitute *archetypes* of male sexuality buried deeply in the collective unconscious of the species.

As an applied interdisciplinary science, *semiotics* enlists such notions only if they are useful for understanding specific signifying phenomena. Indeed, the characteristic trait of semiotic method is the interweaving and blending of ideas, findings, and scientific discourses from other disciplinary domains. In the field of advertising it has forged a partnership with psychology.

Particularly relevant to its objectives are the findings of the *Gestalt* school (German for "configuration"). Gestalt psychology traces its roots to the early work on the relationship between form and content in representational processes by Max Wertheimer (1880-1943), Wolfgang Köhler (1887-1967), and Kurt Koffka (1886-1941), as well as to the work on language conducted by Karl Bühler (1934, 1951) and Ogden and Richards (1923). The two primary objectives of Gestalt psychologists in the study of advertising are:

(1) unraveling how the perception of forms is shaped by the specific contexts in which the forms occur;
(2) investigating how forms interrelate with meanings.

One of the more widely-used techniques in semiotics, known as the *semantic differential*, was actually developed by the Gestalt psychologists Osgood, Suci, and Tannenbaum (1957). This will be discussed in chapter 4. In effect, the partnership between semiotics and psychology has proven to be a very powerful one. It has led to many significant findings.

However, the social debate that the research in psychology has engendered is, as mentioned, something that semioticians should shy away from. Psychologists and social scientists generally ask questions such as the following: Does advertising influence attitudes and behavior? Is it a valuable contributor to the efficiency of a free market economy? Is it a form of artistic expression (note that every year at the Cannes film festival prizes are awarded in the field of advertising)? Such questions have led to a spate of studies that have examined advertising from the broader psychological and cultural perspectives that such questions presuppose.

Perhaps the starting point of the debate can be traced, as mentioned above (1.1.1), to the publication of Vance Packard's 1957 work on the subliminal effects of advertising, *The Hidden Persuaders*, which inspired an outpouring of studies in the 1970s, 1980s, and 1990s examining the effects of advertising on individuals and on society at large (many of the psychological works listed in the bibliography belong to this domain of inquiry). Advertising has also been the target of numerous major analytical, critical, and technical investigations over the same time period (e.g. Vestergaard and Schrøder 1985; Williamson 1985; Beasley, Danesi, and Perron 2000). The implicit question that most of the studies have entertained, without answering it in any definitive fashion, is whether advertising has become a force molding cultural mores and individual behaviors, or whether it constitutes no more than a "mirror" of deeper cultural tendencies within urbanized, contemporary societies. Without going into the debate here, suffice it to say that there is one thing with which virtually everyone agrees - advertising has become one of the most recognizable and appealing forms of social communication to which virtually everyone in society is exposed. The images and messages that advertisers promulgate on a daily basis delineate the contemporary social landscape.

But to what extent are the warnings contained in psychological research papers and monographs on the effects advertising purportedly has on society accurate or justified? Is advertising to be blamed for causing virtually everything, from obesity to street violence? Are media moguls the shapers of behavior that so many would claim they are today? Has advertising spawned the contemporary world? Are the victims of media, as Key (1989: 13) suggests, people who "scream and shout hysterically at rock concerts and later in life at religious revival meetings?" There is no doubt advertising plays a definitive role in shaping some behaviors in some individuals. The highly inflated amount of consumption of fast foods, tobacco, alcohol, and other media-hyped substances is probably related to the slick promotion ploys utilized by magazine ads and television commercials. But, in our view, even though people mindlessly absorb the messages promulgated constantly by advertisements, and although these may have some subliminal effects on behavior, we accept media images, by and large, only if they suit our already-established preferences. It is more accurate to say that advertising produces images that reinforce lifestyle models. Advertisers are not innovators. They are more intent on reinforcing lifestyle behaviors than in spreading commercially-risky innovations. Advertisements are not in themselves disruptive of the value systems of the cultural mainstream; rather, they reflect "shifts" already present in popular culture. If they are indeed psychologically effective, then, as will be argued throughout this book, it is primarily because they tap into deeply-ingrained mythical and metaphorical structures of the mind.

1.3.3 Cognitive style

Following the ideas set forth by McLuhan, it is more accurate, in our opinion, to claim that advertising has affected not *morality* but the *cognitive style* with which people process and understand messages. This was defined by McLuhan (1964) as the mode in which, and the degree to which, the senses are used in processing information. McLuhan pointed out that human beings are endowed by Nature to process information with all the senses. Our *sense ratios*, as he called them, are equally calibrated at birth. However, in social settings it is unlikely that all senses will operate at the same ratio. One sense or the other is raised or lowered according to the representational codes and media deployed. In an oral culture, the *auditory sense ratio* is the operative one; in an alphabetic one, the *visual sense ratio* is raised instead. This raising or lowering of a sense ratio is not preclusive. Indeed, in our own culture, a person can have various sense ratios operating in tandem. The ebb of ratios, up and down, in tandem, in opposition, is what defines the *cognitive style* of information processing.

Now, if anything, advertising has influenced the cognitive style of information processing. It has rendered it much more visual, based on visual images and, thus, more compact and holistic. Unlike traditional narratives (stories, novels, etc.), which have to be processed over a period of time and, thus, require reflection, advertising is immediate, highly visual and synesthetic. This renders the style of information processing much more immediate and much less reflective. And indeed, since the embedding of advertising as a form of social discourse, people have become much more inclined to process information quickly and unreflectively.

1.4 Elements of semiotic analysis

To characterize semiotics as a *science* requires some justification. The question of whether or not human cultures can be studied with the same objectivity as physical matter has always been a problematic one. Indeed, many semioticians refuse to call their field a *science*, since they believe that the study of such phenomena as advertising can never be totally objective. This is why many prefer to define it with terms like "activity," "tool," "doctrine," "theory," "movement," "approach" (Nöth 1990: 4; Sebeok 1990). However, we are in agreement with Umberto Eco (1976), who sees semiotics as a *science* in the traditional sense of the word for five fundamental reasons:

(1) it is an autonomous discipline;
(2) it has a set of standardized methodological tools;
(3) it has the capability of producing hypotheses;
(4) it affords the possibility of making predictions;
(5) its findings may lead to a modification of the actual state of the objective world.

We are, of course, aware that any claim to "scientific objectivity" is to be tempered with caution and wariness. This is not unique to semiotics, however. It has, in fact, become characteristic of all the physical sciences in the twentieth century. Semiotics is indeed an *autonomous discipline*, even if it is interdisciplinary in its overall methodology. In the case of advertising it has, as mentioned, tended to forge a partnership with psychology. But its interdisciplinary scope often encompasses any field that is relevant to its objectives. Mythology, archeology, anthropology, and criticism, for instance, are fields that are frequently enlisted by semioticians in the study of advertising. The *methodological tools* developed by semiotics to study advertising are *standard*. We have already seen some of them used above. Concepts such as *signifier, signified,* and *signification system,* also as we have seen above, can indeed produce *hypotheses* about the phenomena semiotics aims to study and, thus, afford the possibility of making *predictions* vis-à-vis those very phenomena.

1.4.1 Axioms

Every scientific enterprise is constructed on the basis of *axioms*, the primary criteria for distinguishing a scientific enterprise from a non-scientific one established by the ancient Greeks, most probably during the fifth century BC. The axioms of any science must be consistent with one another and few in number.

The axioms that in our view have guided the semiotician's exploration of signifying systems in the past can be summarized as follows:

(1) Cultures the world over are constructed with the same core of sign types and their properties.

(2) This implies that there are universal structures of sense-making in the human species.

(3) Individual cultures are specific instantiations of these structures.

(4) Differences in sign systems result from differences in such instantiations, as caused by human variability and fluctuating contextual-historical factors.

(5) Sign systems entail culture-specific classifications of the world.

(6) These classifications influence the way people think, behave, and act.

(7) Perceptions of "naturalness" are tied to cultural classifications.

Cultural classifications are so deeply rooted in human beings that they can subtly *mediate* how we experience the world. A sign selects what is to be known and memorized from the infinite variety of things that are in the world. Although we create new signs to help us gain new knowledge and modify previous knowledge - this is what artists, scientists, writers, for instance, are always doing - by and large, we literally let our culture "do the understanding" for us. We are born into an already-fixed signifying order that will largely determine how we view the world around us. Only if, hypothetically, all our knowledge (which is maintained in the form of *codes*) were somehow erased from the face of the earth would we need to rely once again on our instinctive meaning-making tendencies to represent the world all over again.

1.4.2 Notions

As Bell (1990: 1) has observed, the semiotic notions used in the study of advertising are powerful because they allow us to bring to the surface the hidden meanings of advertising texts:

> Advertising is all about meaning. In marketing terminology, much advertising research has been concerned with the "message take out" from the commercial. In other words, what did the consumer understand from the commercial? What did it mean? More important than that, how it means.

Consider, again, the case of high heel shoes. The first thing to keep in mind about any advertisement about such shoes is that it is itself a *sign* - something that stands for something else. More specifically, an advertisement is a *text*. We will deal with textuality in subsequent chapters. Suffice it to say here that a *text* is a complex sign made up of various *signifiers* that cohere thematically in the surface structure to weave their underlying *signifieds*. Signifiers such as color tones, the physical appearance of models, the orientation of their bodies, the background scenery, the configuration of the verbal signifiers, etc. are all elements of the surface structure that are perceivable and, thus, analyzable with specific semiotic notions. This includes concepts such as *code, opposition, combination, iconicity, indexicality,* and *symbolicity.*

The colors of the dresses of the models in shoe ads, the color of their hair, the color of the shoes, and so on constitute a *color code,* which is interconnected with a system of the symbolic meanings that colors possess. The basic feature of such codes is *opposition*; i.e. the colors are chosen in such a way as to create a system of contrasting meanings. In the case of, say, white and dark colors used in an ad, the contrast summons forth oppositions such as *good vs. evil, innocence vs. sexuality,* etc. This differentiation relation is known as *paradigmatic structure.* Signification systems cannot be generated in texts without such an oppositional relation between signifiers.

As the elements of an ad enter into a paradigmatic (oppositional) relation with each other, they simultaneously form combinatory and associative patterns. These are known as *syntagmatic* relations. The dark and white colors of an ad are both contrasting and easily combined into syntagmatic patterns: e.g. the white color of a dress is matched perhaps by the pale complexion of the model, the angelic beauty of her face; and so on; the dark color of the shoes may be combined with, say, the model's hair color, her eye color, etc. to imply a "different" side to the story.

Especially useful in the semiotic analysis of advertising are the notions developed by Charles Peirce. Peirce related the connection between signifier and signified (representamen and object) to the vagaries of the human interpreter. Peirce did not, however, view interpretation as necessarily open-ended; but rather that it was potentially infinite. For Peirce, we will always find some new meaning in some context for a sign, no matter how conventionalized the sign's utilization may have become. He called this aspect of the sign the *interpretant.* In a fundamental sense, therefore, the underlying meaning of an ad text can be said to constitute a system of interpretants, since it tends to vary according to individual, context of occurrence, historical period in which it is viewed, etc.

Peirce also provided us with a triadic typology of signs which has now become part of the standard lexicon of semiotic theory and practice. He classified the primary kinds of signs human beings use to represent the world as *icons*, *indexes* and *symbols*. He did not, however, see these as mutually exclusive representational strategies. Signs can, for instance, be partially iconic and symbolic: e.g. the cross in Christian religions stands both for the actual shape of the "cross" on which Christ was crucified (iconic sign) and "Christianity" (symbolic sign) at the same time.

An *icon* is a sign that resembles its referent in some way - e.g. "a pack shot in a commercial stands for the pack" (Bell 1990: 3). In Saussurean terms, it can be defined as a sign in which the signifier is made to look or sound like the signified. Iconicity, as we shall see subsequently, is a primary strategy in advertising. Suggestive shapes, onomatopoeic words, and the like are iconic techniques used to create signification systems for products. Brand names and logos are often iconic. The golden arches of *McDonald's*, for instance (1.1.2), are icons of city arches; the brand name *Acura* is an icon of both a Japanese-sound and an Italian-sounding word (1.1.2); and the list could go on and on.

An *index* is a sign that encodes spatio-temporal or cause-and-effect relations. Smoke is an index of fire; a cough is an index of a cold; and so on. The most typical manifestation of indexicality in advertising is the arrangement of the elements of the surface text of an ad so as to *indicate* either the centrality of the product in the scheme of things or to juxtapose it in relation to the other elements in the text. In some shoe ads the toes of the shoes point indexically to the lettering of the ad. In this way, the product name is highlighted suggestively by indication.

A *symbol* is a sign that has an arbitrary or conventional relation to some referent. Words in general are symbolic signs. The use of symbolism in advertising is, needless to say, ubiquitous, as we shall see in subsequent chapters. The symbolism of a certain type of flower, of a certain kind of shoe, etc. is ultimately what leads to a *decoding* of the underlying signification systems generated by advertisements of all types. In this textbook, we will distinguish between *symbolicity* and *symbolism*. The former is used to refer simply to the employment of symbols in representation (rather than icons or indexes); the later is used to refer instead to the kinds of culture-specific meanings that symbols generate (which are always connotative). Here is a list of a few culture-specific color connotations that show how symbolism works at an unconscious level:

* *white* = purity, innocence, virtuous, chastity, goodness, decency, etc.
* *black* = evil, impurity, guilt, vice, sinfulness, indecency, immorality, etc.
* *red* = passion, sexuality, fertility, fecundity, anger, sensuality, etc.
* *green* = hope, insecurity, naiveté, candor, trust, life, existence, etc.
* *yellow* = liveliness, sunshine, happiness, tranquillity, peacefulness, etc.
* *blue* = sky, paradise, tranquillity, calmness, mysticism, mystery, etc.
* *brown* = earthiness, naturalness, primordiality, constancy, etc.
* *gray* = dullness, mistiness, obscurity, mystery, nebulousness, etc.

When colors are used in an ad text, meanings such as these are the ones that are embedded into the underlying interpretation. The same is true of any code (e.g. the meanings of animals, the meanings of shapes, the meanings of certain figures, the meanings of letters and other kinds of writing symbols, the meanings of numerals, the meaning of sceintific symbols, etc.). Such meanings are rarely obvious because they are unconscious. In effect, they are hardly ever perceived as signs standing for something else; rather tey are perceived as "decorative" or "complementary". This is what makes them very powerful.

The basic notions used in semiotic analysis, with their definitions, can be summarized in table form as follows (table 2):

Table 2.   Summary of the main semiotic notions used in the study of advertising

Notion	Definition
signifier	the perceivable (visible, audible, etc.) part of the sign
signified	the meaning evoked, or the referent captured, by a signifier
signification system	the system of meanings generated by the association of signifiers with certain signifieds (creating connotative chains)
opposition/paradigmaticity	the meaning contrasts produced by certain signifiers in a text in order to generate a signification system
combination/syntagmaticity	the meanings produced by combinations of signifiers in a text in order to generate a signification system
code	the inbuilt system of cultural meanings built into a sign, text, etc.
iconicity	the property of signs by which signifiers are made to resemble their signifieds in some perceivable fashion
indexicality	the property of signs by which signifiers point out the location, relation, etc. of signifieds
symbolicity	the property of signs by which signifiers stand for signifieds according to cultural convention or tradition
symbolism	the kinds of meanings generated by symbols according to cultural convention, history, or tradition
text	a complex sign made up of multiple signifiers and signifieds
surface level	the physically perceivable part of an ad text
underlying level	the hidden level of meaning of an ad text; also called the *subtext*

1.4.3 Meaning

The remaining notions that are used frequently in the semiotic analysis of advertising all deal with the nature of *meaning*. This is a problematic term for semioticians; for this reason, it is the standard practice to differentiate between *meaning* and *signification*. The former is used generally in semiotics in its broad dictionary definition of "anything that is intended," or "anything of some value to human beings." Incidentally, this leads to a semantic circularity that cannot be avoided. In their 1923 work, titled appropriately *The Meaning of Meaning*, Ogden and Richards gave 23 meanings of the word *meaning*, showing how problematic a term it is. Here are some of them:

- He *means* to write   =   "intends"
- A green light *means* go   =   "indicates"
- Health *means* everything   =   "has importance"
- Her look was full of *meaning* =   "special import"
- Does life have a *meaning*?   =   "purpose"
- What does love *mean* to you?   =   "convey"

In effect, the term *meaning* defies definition. Like the basic axioms of Euclidean geometry, it is best left as a notion of which everyone has an intuitive understanding, but which cannot itself be explained in absolute terms. It is a semiotic *given*. The term *signification* is much easier to define, even though *meaning* and *signification* are often used interchangeably by many semioticians. Essentially, *signification* designates the particular thoughts and responses that a sign evokes. *Signification* is not an open-ended process, however; it is constrained by a series of factors, including conventional agreements as to what a sign means in specific contexts, the type of *code* to which it belongs, the nature of its referents - concrete referents are less subject to variation than are abstract ones - and so on. Without such inbuilt constraints, signification and communication would be virtually impossible in common social settings.

Ogden and Richards also made a key distinction between *meaning* on the one side, and *sense* and *reference* on the other. *Sense* alludes etymologically to the physical nature of meaning. A sign must be received and perceived by our "biological sensors," so to speak, before it can have any "meaning" in the first place. At this basic level, meaning is anchored in a *sensory* reaction to the content represented in the sign. *Reference*, on the other hand, is the process by which our sense reactions and thoughts are connected to reality through the use of signs within sign systems (or *codes*).

It is obvious that the use of signs to create messages and meanings entails an *interpretation* of what they mean. Since this is always bound to create controversy, because the range of interpretations always varies from individual to individual, the reader should be aware, therefore, of the fact that all the "interpretations" put forward in this book are subject to our own subjective responses to advertisements. The reader may or may not agree with our interpretive proposals, may see more into an advertisement along the suggested lines of interpretation, or may see nothing at all in it. This is a normal feature of interpretation. There is no one meaning that can be extracted from a human-made text. The purpose of this book is not to impose a set of specific interpretations on the reader, but to illustrate an analytical methodology that indicates exactly how multifarious modes of interpretation are intentionally built into advertising.

The sign's primary meaning is called its *denotation*. This is the meaning or referential connection established between signifier and signified. But this meaning can be extended freely to other domains of reference. This extensive process is known as *connotation*. Consider the word *house*. Its denotation can be paraphrased as "any structure for human habitation." The denotative uses of this sign can be seen in utterances such as the following:

- I bought a new *house* yesterday.

- *House* prices are continually going up in this city.

- We repainted our *house* the other day.

But, by connotative extension, the same sign can be used to mean such things as a "legislative assembly" ("The *house* is in session at this moment"), "audience" ("The *house* roared with laughter"), etc. Note, however, that the basic elements of the sign's denotative meaning must be present in its extended uses for *signification* to be successful. So, in the above sentences the denotative signifieds "structure," "human," and "habitation" are necessarily implicit in the connotative uses: a legislative assembly and a theater audience do indeed imply "structures" of special kinds that "humans" can be said to "inhabit." Any connotative utilization of the word *house* is constrained by this "minimal structure;" i.e. the word-sign *house* can be applied to refer to anything that involves or implicates humans coming together for some specific reason.

As Barthes correctly pointed out, the notion of *connotation* is of great importance to the study of advertisements, because it constitutes a "fund of knowledge" of a particular culture into which a sign taps. Specific colors at certain times of the year, for instance, connote traditions, values, and belief systems. In our culture *white* is often symbolic of "cleanliness," "purity," "innocence," whereas *dark*, its paradigmatic counterpart, symbolizes "uncleanness," "impurity," "corruption." The remainder of this book is, in effect, a study of how *connotation* is utilized in the field of advertising. Digging deeper into the connotative symbolism of ads, it will be seen that the paradigmatic contrast of two colors, say *white* and *black*, suggests a connotative struggle between *innocence* and something more *sinister*. Mythic connotation is a powerful component of the unconscious mind.

The philosopher Susanne Langer (1948) convincingly argued over half a century ago that, at a primary level of mind, we apprehend the world through "feeling;" i.e. we "feel" that the world has a structure. She called this the *presentational* form of cognition. When we attempt to explain our feeling states vis-à-vis some event or representation (such as a work of art), we are forced to reorganize it in terms of language and its linear semiotic structures. She called this the discursive form of cognition. This is a *re-presentational* form of thinking that will never be able to cover the entire range of presentational effects produced by a meaningful stimulus or text.

The strategies of advertising - brand naming, logo creation, package design, ad textuality, etc. - work at a presentational level first. We react to them in terms of feeling. It is when we attempt an explanation of a brand name, a logo, a magazine ad, etc. that we enter into a discursive mode of interpretation, subject to the constraints of the particular language being used. But, then, this is inevitable in any interpretive venture: in literary criticism, musicology, art aesthetics, etc. Hermeneutics, or the art of interpretation, is invariably a discursive technique that can never be objective and absolute. Indeed, in our view, the interesting and significant aspect of hermeneutics is that it allows ample space for differences in the interpretation of any artifact, symbol, or text, opening up a potentially fertile dialectic on its meaning. The next three chapters are, in effect, our own "hermeneutic excursions" into the domain of meanings generated by advertising techniques. Hopefully, these will engage the reader in a dialectic with us or, at the very least, lead him or her to reflect on the kinds of signification systems generated by advertising.

1.4.4 Case-in-point 2: An ad for a sparkling wine

To get a concrete grasp of how ads generate meaning, it is instructive to analyze a lifestyle ad chosen at random from a magazine. For this purpose, we have selected an ad for *Marilyn Peach*, a sparkling wine, that was found in many European magazines a few years ago. This ad cannot be reproduced here for reasons of copyright. It can only be described verbally. The surface text shows a peach background which appears to match both the color and the taste of the wine. At the underlying level, however, the idea that comes to mind is that of the dawn which, in turn, suggests the Genesis narrative (the dawn of creation, the dawn of life). Several surface level features bear this out - we see a woman's hand holding out a drinking glass of the wine, offering it temptingly to someone; the woman is wearing a bracelet in the form of a snake. Now, in the Book of Genesis the devil came to Eve in the body of a snake to prod her on to tempt Adam. A male partner is probably the one who is being seductively offered the glass. Will he take it? Well, like the Biblical Adam, how can he resist? If one still has doubts about this narrative interpretation, the accompanying French verbal text - *La pêche, le nouveau fruit de la tentation* ("Peach, the new fruit of temptation") - will undoubtedly dispel them.

Whether or not this ad will induce consumers to buy *Marilyn Peach* is open to question. As mentioned several times in this chapter, it is certainly not the point of semiotic analysis to determine this. The point of the above analysis was simply to illustrate the method of semiotic analysis itself, not to provide a definitive interpretation of the ad. The key to unlocking the underlying mythic meaning is to consider the surface signifiers in a sequence, just like a comic strip, in order to see where the sequence leads in the subtext. As mentioned previously (1.2.1), this technique can be called *connotative chaining* because each signifier evokes a connotation which in turn evokes another, and then another after that, and so on. This notion will be taken up at length in subsequent chapters. Suffice it to say here that in the *Marilyn Peach* ad the *connotative chain* goes somewhat like this:

> *the peach background = dawn = dawn of creation = Garden of Eden scene = Eve tempting Adam = prodded on by a serpent (on the bracelet) = he who drinks the wine will yield to temptation (La pêche, le nouveau fruit de la tentation)*

In most lifestyle ads, the mythic subtext can be wrested from such connotative chains, which are often reinforced by the visual and verbal signifiers in the surface text - e.g. by the shape of the product, by shadows and colors, by the name of the product, etc.

Chapter II
Creating recognizability for the product

Ideally, advertising aims at the goal of a programmed harmony among all human impulses and aspirations and endeavors. Using handicraft methods, it stretches out toward the ultimate electronic goal of a collective consciousness..

Marshall McLuhan (1911–1980)

2. Introductory remarks

The three primary strategies used today to enhance product recognizability, in line with the *law* of the marketplace, are known generally as *repetition, positioning, image-creation. Repetition* is a basic marketing technique. A typical national advertiser can capture the attention of prospective customers by repeated appeals to buy some product through sales talks on radio and television, advertisements for the same product in newspapers and magazines, and poster displays in stores and elsewhere (on subway panels, buses, etc.). *Positioning* (1.1.2) is the targeting of a product through appropriate advertising for the right audience of consumers - e.g. *Chanel* products are positioned for a female audience of a certain social class; *Nike* shoes for a trendy adolescent and young adult audience; *Audis* and *BMWs* for an up-scale class of consumers; *Dodge* vans for a middle-class suburban consumer population; and so on. Positioning is likewise a fundamental marketing strategy. The creation of an *image* for a product is accomplished by generating a signification system for it that renders it appealing to specific types of consumers (1.1.2). *Budweiser* beer, for instance, evokes a signification system consisting of such signifieds as "ruggedness," "athletics," "male bonding," "fun;" whereas *Heineken* evokes a system consisting of such signifieds as "smoothness" and "sophistication." This is why commercials for *Budweiser* are positioned next to sports events on television, and why those for *Heineken* are found primarily in next to more "culturally sensitive" programs on TV.

A signification system is, obviously, one constructed on the basis of socially based connotations. For example, the *State Farm* insurance company has established such a system for itself through the use of four main representational techniques (Beasley, Danesi, and Perron 2000):

(1) a brand name (*State Farm*) that can be associated with "down-to-earth" (agrarian, country, rural) values, especially friendliness and trustworthiness;

(2) a logo made up of geometric figures that communicates order and symmetry and, thus, a sense of assurance;

(3) a jingle (*Like a good neighbor, State Farm is there*) that reiterates and reinforces these signifieds;

(4) ads and commercials portraying *State Farm* employees as wholesome, neighborly individuals ready to help out in time of need.

From this signification system an *image* of the *State Farm* company as a "friendly" and "trustworthy" institution has crystallized over the years, becoming fixed in the social mindset through repeated advertising campaigns.

This chapter has two objectives:

(1) to briefly describe some of the basic representational techniques that are used to generate signification systems for enhancing product recognizability;

(2) to discuss how recognizability and image are established through various media and ad campaigns.

2.1 Creating a signification system

To create a signification system for a product it is necessary, above all else, to give it a *name* and, whenever possible, to assign it a visual representation known as a *logo*. By assigning it a name, the product, like any person, can now be recognized in terms of its name. This guarantees it a high degree of recognizability. The truth of this principle can be seen in the fact that most readers will easily recognize a large portion of the following list of products, commodities, and services selected at random from lists provided by consumer information agencies:

Arrid	*Ban*
Banana Republic	*Barbie Dolls*
Ben-Gay	*Budweiser*
Bufferin	*Cheerios*
Clairol	*Clorets*
Coca-Cola	*Crest*
Doritos	*Dristan*
Eveready Batteries	*Fab Detergent*
Folger's Coffee	*Fruitopia Drinks*
Gatorade	*Ivory Soap*
Jack Daniel's	*Jell-O*
Kleenex	*Kool-Aid*
Krazy Glue	*Listerine*
Marlboro Cigarettes	*Maxwell House Coffee*
Miller Beer	*Monopoly*
Noxema	*Pampers*
Playtex	*Quaker Oats*
Ritz Crackers	*Rolaids*
Schick Razors	*Scotch Tape*
The Gap	*Tylenol*
Victoria's Secret	*Zest Soap*

These have become, literally, house-hold names because they have a high recognizability index. No wonder, then, that *trademarks* - which is the legal term for *brand name* - are so fiercely protected by corporations and manufacturers. This is what allows consumers to identify their goods and distinguish them from those made or sold by others. The brand name identifies the source of a product and fixes responsibility for its quality. So powerful is the brand name as an identifier of the product that, on several occasions, it has instead been used by consumers as metonyms to name the product type. Such names then lost their legal status as trademarks. Examples include *aspirin*, *cellophane*, and *escalator*.

In each industrialized country anyone who uses a trademark or logo acquires the legal right to prevent others from subsequently using a similar mark. Anyone who uses a mark so similar to a registered one that it is likely to cause customer confusion is considered generally to be an infringer and can be sued. Unlike patent or copyright infringement, trademark infringement is defined solely by the likely confusion of customers. The usual remedy after a court trial finding trademark infringement is an injunction prohibiting the infringer from using its mark. Again, all this bears witness to the power of brand names as primary constituents in the product's signification system.

2.1.1 Brand names

In the previous chapter (1.2.1), we discussed briefly the fact that a signification system for a product is sometimes generated by building it into the physical structure of the brand name itself. The name *Acura*, as we saw, was designed to be imitative of the shape of an Italian word. By metaphorical extension, this brand is linked to the perceived qualities of the Italian language and its speakers. This must be an effective strategy because, as can be seen from the list below, car makers, have used this exact same strategy of creating car names ending in the vowel -*a* which, given their inbuilt melodious quality, are probably easier to remember, sound aesthetically pleasing, and, thus, bestow an artistic quality onto the perception of the automobile:

Acura
Asuna
Altima
Achieva
Aurora
Festiva
Integra
Elantra

Precidia
Maxima
Sonata
Samara
Serenia
Sentra
Lumina
Corsica

Carmakers have also started looking at more trendy naming trends that appeal to a generation of Internet users who have become accustomed to abbreviations in their style of communication. Cadillac, for instance, announced a new model with the monogram name CTS in 2001. Names using just letters and numbers have, in fact, become the rage. Acura itself has introduced a new line of models with names such as: TL, RL, MDX, RSX. Such "alphabetic names" evoke images of technology and sleekness and, more significantly, they are consistent with "Internet grammar," which can be called simply "Internetese," a telegraphic form of communication that spawns monogrammatic and alphanumeric signifiers on a daily basis. Hyundai's XG300 model, for instance, sounds perfect for the times - and sales back up its popularity. On the other side of the naming equation, such abbreviations are hard to remember, especially for older customers who have not yet tapped into Internetese.

Here are other examples of how brand names are constructed to generate specific kinds of signification systems:

Many names refer simply to the actual manufacturer/company indicating "tradition," "reliability," etc., and in the case of lifestyle products "artistry, "sophistication," etc.:

Bell
Armani
Benetton
Kraft
Gillette

Folger's
etc.

Some names refer to a fictitious personality, thus eliciting images associated with the name itself (e.g. *Wendy's* evokes the image a friendly young girl):

McDonald's
Wendy's
Aunt Jemima
Mr. Clean
etc.

A number of names simply identify the geographical location of the company/manufacturer:

American Bell
Southern Bell
etc.

Many names refer to some aspect of Nature, so as to bestow upon the product the images that Nature elicits:

Tide
Surf
Cascade
Aqua Velva
Mountain Dew
etc.

This is particularly so with the naming of sport-utility vehicles and pickups for which "Wild West: names are the norm:

Jeep Grand Cherokee
Jeep Wrangler
Jeep Renegade

Hyundai Santa Fe
Ford Explorer
Ford Expedition
Ford Escape
Mercury Moutaineer
Dodge Durango

Some names are constructed as hyperboles to emphasize product "superiority," "excellence," etc.:

MaxiLight
SuperFresh
UltraLite
etc.

Constructing brand names as combinations of words is a strategy intended simply to describe the product:

Fruitopia (= Fruit + Utopia)
Yogourt (= Yogurt + Gourmet)
Frogurt (= Frozen + Yogurt)
etc.

Many names are designed to show what the product can do:
Easy On
Lestoil
One Wipe
Quick Flow
Easy Wipe
etc.

And various names are designed to show what can be accomplished with the product:

Bug Off
Close-Up Toothpaste

Air Fresh
No Sweat
etc.

Brand names, thus, typically do more than just identify a product. As the above examples show, they are typically constructed to create signification systems for the product. Most of the above names elicited largely denotative meanings: i.e. they identified the manufacturer (*Bell, Kraft*, etc.), they indicated the geographical location of the company (*Southern Bell, American Bell*, etc.) they conveyed what the product can do *Easy On, Quick Flow*, etc.), and so on and so forth. Nevertheless, even in relaying straightforward information, such names still have the signifying power of associated meanings that any name elicits. The name *Bell*, for instance, evokes meanings of "tradition," "reliance," etc. that familiarity with the name has projected onto its signified. In effect, there is virtually no sign used in a cultural context that does not entail connotation. So, by claiming that the signification systems above are denotative, we are simply intedning to convey that their primary intent is to provide information of a practical nature.

Several of the brand names, however, were designed, as we saw, to elicit mainly connotative arrays of meanings - the names referring to Nature (*Tide, Surf, Cascade*, etc.), the names referring to fictitious personalities (*McDonald's, Wendy's, Aunt Jemima*, etc.), and the names fashioned as hyperboles (*MaxiLite, SuperFresh*, etc.) all evoked such arrays. Generating connotative meanings is, in fact, a typical strategy of brand naming (Javed 1993). This bestows upon the product's image much more than a simple denotative or identification system. It creates a semiotically-powerful signification system for it that can be used and reused for various advertising purposes. Indeed, the more connotations a name evokes, the more powerful it is and, as a consequence, the more possibilities it offers to the advertiser for creating truly effective ads and commercials. The higher the "connotative index" of a signification system, the greater its market effectiveness.

Below are just a few examples of how connotative signification systems are generated by the type of name used (table 3):

Table 3. Signification systems associated with certain brand names

Brand Names	Signification Systems
Superpower, Multicorp, Future Now, Quantum Health Resources, PowerAde, etc.	"big picture," "forward-looking," "strong," "powerful," etc.
People's Choice, Advantage Plus, Light N' Easy, Viewer's Choice, etc.	"free-spirited," "advantageous," egalitarian," "common," "friendly," etc.
Biogenical, Technics, Panasonic, Vagisil, Anusol, Proof Positive, Timex, etc.	"scientific," "methodical," "fool-proof," "accurate," "reliable," etc.
Coronation, Morning Glory, Burger King, Monarch's Flour, etc.	"conquering," "regal," "majesty," "nobility," "blue-blooded," etc.
Wash 'N Wear, Drip-Dry, Easy Clean, Okay Plus, etc.	"user-friendly," "simple," "uncomplicated," "basic," etc.
General Electric, General Mills, General Dynamics, General Foods, etc.	"all-encompassing" "widespread," "popular," etc.
Cheer, Joy, etc.	"happy," "bright," "friendly," "smiling," etc.
Pledge, Promise, etc.	"trustworthy," "reliant," "secure," etc.

At a practical, informational level, naming a product has a *denotative* function, i.e. it allows consumers to identify what product they desire to purchase (or not). But at a *connotative* level the product's name generates images that go well beyond this simple identifier function. Consider *Gucci* shoes as a case-in-point. Denotatively, the name allows us to identify the shoes, should we desire to buy them. However, this is not all it does. The use of the manufacturer's name, rather than some invented name or expression, assigns an aura of craftsmanship and superior quality to the product. The shoes can thus be perceived to be the "work" of an artist (the manufacturer). They constitute a "work of shoe art," so to speak, not just an assembly-line product for everyone to wear.

This is a widely used strategy in the area of brand naming life-style products. In the fashion industry, *designer* names such as *Gucci*, *Armani*, and *Calvin Klein* evoke images of *objets d'art*, rather than images of mere clothes, shoes, or jewelry; so too do names such as *Ferrari*, *Lamborghini*, and *Maserati* in the domain of automobiles. The manufacturer's name, in such cases, *extends* the denotative meaning of the product considerably. This extensional process is known, of course, as connotation. The signification system created to ensconce product image into the social mindset is a *de facto* connotative one. When people buy an *Armani* or a *Gucci* product, for instance, they feel that they are buying a work of art to be displayed on the body; when they buy *Poison*, by *Christian Dior*, they sense that they are buying a dangerous, but alluring, love potion; when they buy *Moondrops, Natural Wonder, Rainflower, Sunsilk,* or *Skin Dew* cosmetics they feel that they are acquiring some of Nature's beauty resources; and when they buy *Eterna 27, Clinique, Endocil,* or *Equalia* beauty products they sense that they are getting products imbued with scientific validity. *No-name* products do not engender such systems of connotations.

Connotations of "sexuality" and "eroticism" are typically part of the signification system that high heel shoes evoke, as we saw in the previous chapter (1.2.3). These meanings derive from the fact that *high heel* shoes are perceived as sexy and, thus, to be worn only by mature women (not young girls). At a denotative level a *shoe* can be defined simply as "a durable covering for the human foot." It is something that makes locomotion much more endurable than walking barefoot. This denotative signified can be seen in utterances such as:

- I bought a new pair of *shoes* yesterday.

- *Shoe* prices are continually going up in this city.

- We threw out our old *shoes* the other day.

But, by connotative extension, the *type* of shoes one wears carries along with it certain social *connotations*. High heel shoes have a long history of association with eroticism, as we saw. This is why we talk of *shoe fetishes* and why erotic depictions of females seem to be more sexually enticing when high heel shoes are worn than when they are not. If the high heel shoes are made by *Gucci*, then wearing them entails, additionally, wearing "a work of erotic shoe art."

The overall configuration of such signifieds creates a signification system for this product that can be schematized as follows:

High Heel Shoes by Gucci

Denotation	Extensional Connotation	Social Connotation
the brand name allows us to identify the product for shopping purposes	being the actual name of the manufacturer, the brand name allows us to feel that we are buying a work of shoe art	since high heel shoes evoke an erotic image, they are perceived to be a work of *erotic* shoe art

Figure 2. Signification system for *Gucci* high heel shoes

Incidentally, *branding* was, originally, the searing of flesh with a hot iron to produce a scar or *mark* with an easily recognizable pattern for identification or other purposes. Livestock were branded by the Egyptians as early as 2000 BC. In the late medieval period, trades people and guild members posted characteristic *marks* outside their shops, leading to the notion of *trademark* (mentioned above). Medieval swords and ancient Chinese pottery, for instance, were also marked with identifiable symbols so buyers could trace their origin and determine their quality. Among the best-known trademarks surviving from early modern times are the striped pole of the barbershop and the three-ball sign of the pawnbroker shop.

Names were first used towards the end of the nineteenth century when many American firms began to market packaged goods under such names. Previously, everyday household products were sold in neighborhood stores from large bulk containers. Around 1880, soap manufacturers started naming their products so that they could be identified. The first modern-day *brand names* were thus invented. They included:

> *Ivory*
> *Pears'*
> *Sapolio*
> *Colgate*
> *Kirk's American Family*
> *Packer's*

Soon afterward, other manufacturers joined the bandwagon, adding names such as the following to the growing list of products that were being identified with brand names:

> *Royal Baking Powder*
> *Quaker Oats*
> *Baker's Chocolate*
> *Hire's Root Beer*
> *Regal Shoes*
> *Waterman's Pens*
> *Bon Ami*
> *Wrigley*
> *Coca-Cola*

As Naomi Klein (2000: 6) aptly observes, the early period of branding became the general practice among manufacturers of products because the market was starting to be flooded by uniform mass-produced and, thus, indistinguishable products: "Competitive branding became a necessity of the machine age." By the early 1950s, it became obvious that branding was not just a simple strategy for product differentiation, but the very fuel that propelled corporate identity and product recognizability. Even the advent of "no-name" products, designed to cut down the cost of buying them to the consumer, have had little effect on the power that branding has on the consciousness of people. Names like *Nike, Apple, Body Shop, Calvin Klein, Levi's,* etc. have become intrinsic signs of the cultural order, recognized by virtually anyone living in a modern-day society. As

Klein (2000: 16) goes on to remark, for such firms the brand name constitutes "the very fabric of their companies."

2.1.2 Logos

Logos (an abbreviation of *logogriphs*), are the pictorial counterparts of brand names. They are used to generate the same kinds of connotative signification systems for a product, typically in a complementary fashion.

Consider the apple logo adopted by the *Apple Computer* company. This is, clearly, charged with latent religious connotations, suggesting the story of Adam and Eve in the Western Bible, which revolves around the eating of an apple that was supposed to embody secret forbidden knowledge. In actual fact, the Hebrew account of the Genesis story tells of a "forbidden" fruit, not specifically of an apple. The representation of this fruit as an apple came about in medieval depictions of the Eden scene, when painters and sculptors became interested in the Genesis story artistically. In the Koran, on the other hand, the forbidden fruit is a banana. Now, the Biblical symbolism of the apple as "forbidden knowledge" continues to resonate in our culture. This is why the *Apple* computer company has not only named itself with the word *Apple*, but has also chosen the picture of this fruit as its logo, symbolizing the fact that it, too, provides "forbidden" knowledge to those who buy and use its products. Incidentally, the logo shows an apple that has had a bite taken from it, thus reinforcing the link between the logo and the Genesis story by associating the use of *Apple* computers and products with Eve, the mother of humanity.

The power of the visual sign is what makes the logo so much an intrinsic feature today of product recognizability. Until the 1970s, logos on clothes were concealed discretely inside a collar or on a pocket. But since then, they are displayed prominently, becoming true symbols imbued with endless arrays of meanings. *Ralph Lauren's* polo horseman, *Lacoste's* alligator, and the like are now worn proudly to demonstrate adherence to a kind of heraldic signification system. They constitute symbols of "cool" (Klein 2000: 69), that legions of adolescents are eager to put on display in order to show conformity to peer-based perceptions of fashionableness.

2.1.3 Iconicity

Brand names and logos that are made to reproduce or simulate some aspect of the products they represent are particularly effective in enhancing the product's recognizability. Such forms are known as *icons*, as we saw in the previous chapter (1.3.2). The *Apple* computer logo mentioned above is an example of a visual icon, because it portrays its referent (an "apple") visually. A name such as *Ritz Crackers* is an example of an of audio-oral icon, since it assigns a sonority to the product that is simulative of sounds that crackers can be perceived to make as they are being eaten.

Iconicity is a common representational strategy in all areas of advertising, from product manufacturing itself to brand name and creation of ad texts. Commercially produced perfumes that are suggestive of natural scents are iconic in an olfactory way, because they have been manufactured to simulate natural scents. Onomatopoeic jingles - *Plop, plop, fizz, fizz, Snap, crackle, pop*, etc. - are iconic in an auditory way, because they simulate the sounds made by the products they represent. The choice by the *Guy Laroche* company of the name *Drakkar noir* for one of its cologne products, along with the pitch-dark appearance of the cologne bottle, are respectively acoustic and visual iconic forms. The bottle has a ghastly, frightful black color, connoting fear, evil, the unknown. Forbidden things also take place under the cloak of the dark night; hence the name *noir* (French for "black"). The sepulchral name of the cologne, *Drakkar noir*, is transparently congruous with the bottle's design at a connotative level, reinforcing the idea that something dark, scary, but nevertheless desirous, happen by splashing on the cologne. The guttural *Drakkar* is also suggestive of *Dracula*, the deadly vampire who mesmerized his sexual prey with a mere glance.

2.2 Creating textuality

The signification systems that result from assigning names and logos and products is what permits advertisers to create effective ad and commercial texts. The basic characteristic of such texts is, in fact, that they embed this system into their very make-up in highly creative ways. Recall the *Marilyn Peach* ad discussed briefly in the previous chapter (1.4.4). The main elements of the surface text are as follows:

- a peach colored background;

- this matches both the color and the taste of the wine (= syntagmatic structure);

- a woman's hand is holding out a drinking glass of the wine;

- she is clearly offering it temptingly to someone;

- the woman is wearing a bracelet in the form of a snake;

- the verbal text is: *La pêche, le nouveau fruit de la tentation*

This text has, in effect, translated in visual and verbal form the connotations of the *Marilyn Peach* signification system, creating a subtext that can be interpreted as a page out of the Bible. As already mentioned, in the Book of Genesis the devil came to Eve in the body of a snake to incite her on to tempt Adam. But her fruit was an *apple;* the *peach* fruit used in making the wine is now the *nouveau fruit de la tentation.* The underlying sexuality of the whole narrative scene is emphasized by the very nature of the *peach* - a highly erotic succulent fruit, that is highly suggestive of female genitalia. Extending the signification system into this erotic domain, the whole ad can simultaneously be linked to the perception of women in Western culture as "temptresses."

Note that these elements cohere into a system of meaning that leads to a *narrative* interpretation of the text based on the Biblical story of Adam and Eve. Is the *Marilyn Peach* ad text truly a modern representation of this ancient Biblical text? The answer would seem to be *yes.* Incidentally, the tactile feeling of the peach associated with a visual image - the orange background (the "dawn" of creation) is highly synesthetic. In all synesthetic experiences, the imagination takes over the functions of perception. This tends to produce an overall mixing sensory modalities to produce a pleasant feeling called *aesthesia*, defined as a total sensory and affective response to a text.

Incidentally, the symbol of the *peach* is found in other signification systems developed for other products. Berger (2000: 59-60) found it in an ad for a moisturizer called *Living Proof Cream Hidracel* that is accompanied by a large headline that reads as follows:

> *There is a fountain of youth.*
> *It's called water.*

> *Nature has been telling us this forever. Water keeps a rose fresh and beautiful. A peach juicy. All living things, living. Including your skin. The millions of cells in your skin contain water. This water pillows and cushions your skin, making it soft and young-looking. But, for a lot of reasons, cells become unable to hold water. And the water escapes your skin. (If you'll forgive us, think of a prune drying up and you'll know the whole story.)*

First, note that the headline reads like a scientific textbook, giving it a flavor of "authoritativeness" and "objectivity." The actual text promises to help women remain young and avoid "drying up" like prunes. The phrase "*A peach juicy*" is an interpretive key to the ad's connotative level. Having *peachlike* skin, by "moistening" it has, as Berger suspects, a connection with fertility. This connotation of a peach as "moist" and thus highly erotic *object of desire* is the same type of connotation embedded in the *Marilyn Peach* ad.

The same signification system was built into the brand name *Pango Peach*, a color introduced by Revlon in 1960. This is why advertisements about this color invariably described its use in highly erotic ways (Berger 2000: 61). In all promotions of this product one found expressions such as:

- pink with pleasure
- a volcano of color
- fullripe peach

- succulent on your lips
- sizzling on your fingertips

These are all suggestive, metaphorically, of female genitalia. At the same time, they are evocative of the gustatory reactions that ensue from eating a peach. Either way, the synesthetic effects embedded in such phrases make it obvious that the *peach* is a symbol of femininity, sexuality, eroticism, youth, and beauty at once.

The *textuality* generated by ads and commercials - i.e. the specific mode or modes of making advertisements and commercials on the basis of specific signification systems built intentionally into products - is an intrinsic feature of advertising method. The textuality created for products can also be reinforced by slogans and jingles. The *Plop, plop, fizz, fizz, oh what a relief it is!* jingle for *Alka-Seltzer*, the *Snap, Crackle,* and *Pop* jingle for *Rice Crispies* are just two examples of how jingles and products can become intertwined textually. These typically impart a friendly, often humorous, quality to the product's image. Classical music can likewise be worked into a product's textuality to convey a sense of superiority and high-class aspirations. For instance, in the Ontario-based milk advertising campaign, *Drink milk, love life!* of the late 1990s (in which the authors of this manual were involved), the use of the *Ode to Joy* section of the fourth movement of Ludwig van Beethoven's (1770-1827) ninth symphony was added as an integral component of the product's textuality to impart a sense of joy to the drinking of milk by emphasizing the uplifting qualities of milk through the uplifting feeling evoked by the music. Creating characters on purpose to become the main protagonists in the product's textuality - e.g. *Speedy (Alka-Seltzer), Ronald McDonald (McDonald's), Tony the Tiger (Esso), Ronald McDonald (McDonald's),* etc. - or by having the product endorsed by famous personages - actors, sports figures, etc. are other ways in which the product's recognizability index is enhanced.

2.2.1 Features of ad texts

The creation of a textuality for a product ensures that the connotative signifieds associated with its image are given a certain stability over time. As Diane Barthel (1988: 18) aptly puts it, this creates a stable *personality* for the product:

> Would-be advertising men are advised that the one word consumers never tire of is *me*. Advertisers simply tell them who that "me" is, and how to make it ever more attractive, comfortable, exciting, appealing. To do this, advertisers must do more than communicate information on a product. They must communicate image. Their task is somehow to position a product within a market of competing goods and to aim it toward an identifiable population. They must give it a personality.

What changes in specific textual representations of the product are the signifiers that deliver the same signifieds. Thus, for example, the *Marilyn Peach* ad, which goes back a number of years, could be updated by changing such signifiers as the look of the temptress and the style of her "offering." The new signifiers could then be organized to represent a more contemporary "view" of temptation in updated versions of the ad. The underlying mythic story could also be changed to reflect some other narrative portrayal of feminine sexuality (e.g. the myth of Diana, of Aphrodite, of Persephone, etc.), rather than that of Eve. But the signification system would remain essentially the same.

Returning to Barthes' idea of neomania (1.2), it can be said that the craving for new things is generated not only by changing some manufacturing detail (e.g. adding more or less sugar in the make-up of the wine, increasing its alcohol content, etc.), but also by constantly updating the signifiers that deliver its textuality in ads and commercials. This is also a basic strategy for maintaining consumer loyalty. People seem to like the same things, with their constant meanings, but they also want to make sure that they are "in style," or "up to date," in what they buy.

The word *text*, as it is used in semiotic theory, means something very specific. It literally designates a "putting together" of signifiers to produce a message, consciously or unconsciously. The text can be either verbal or nonverbal, or both. In order for the text to signify something, one must know the *code* or *codes* to which the signifiers used belong. What does this imply? Consider the following simple example. If one were to listen to a verbal language that one does not know, all one would hear are "disembodied signifiers" - sounds, intonations, etc. that one intuitively knows cohere into words and phrases that carry some intended meaning, but to which one has no access. The "embodiment" of the verbal signifiers - i.e. their linkage to meaning - occurs only when one comes to know the language *code* to which they belong (its phonetic system, its grammar, its lexicon, etc.). Similarly, musical performances, stage plays, common discourse exchanges, dance styles, religious rites, ceremonies, etc. are texts that we regularly make, as individuals or groups, from the various codes that a culture puts at our disposal. Access to the meanings generated by such texts is possible only if the codes used to create them are known.

As Roger Schank (1984: 125) points out, codes allow us to understand all such textualities because they constitute systems for storing the knowledge structures that underlie human activities. This is why texts often appear to us as being "script-like:"

> When we read a story, we try to evaluate the reasoning processes of the main character. We try to determine why he does what he does and what he will do next. We examine what we would do in a similar situation, and we try to make the same connections that the main character seems to be making. We ask ourselves, What is he trying to do? What's his plan? Why did he do what he just did? Any understanding system has to be able to decipher the reasoning processes that actors in stories go through. Sometimes people achieve their goals by resorting to a script. When a script is unavailable, that is, when the situation is in some way novel, people are able to make up new plans.

To the notion of code in advertising, Barthes (1977) added the concept of *anchorage*, or the notion that visual images in advertisements are polysemous (i.e. the have many meanings), which are anchored by viewers to specific socially meaningful texts (e.g. the Bible, ancient mythical stories, etc.). Ad texts are constructed with signifiers that imply an endless chain of signifieds from which the viewer can choose some and ignore others: i.e. the text's signifieds are anchored to specific signification systems by specific interpreters.

In the modern theory of texts, the underlying, connotative meaning on which a text is anchored is commonly referred to as its *subtext*. The incorporation of other textualities present in the culture, through direct citation or indirect allusion, is called *intertextuality*. Consider, again the *Marilyn Peach* ad. It is obvious that its subtextual meaning of *Biblical* temptation is anchored a chain of connotative signifieds:

> *the peach background = dawn = dawn of creation = Garden of Eden scene = Eve tempting Adam = prodded on by a serpent (bracelet) = he who drinks the wine will yield to temptation = etc.*

This interpretation would be literally "meaningless" in cultures that do not ascribe the same connotative meaning to snakes or the dawn. In other words, the interpretation of a text's subtextual signification system is anchored in both the interpreter and in the specific culture in which the interpretation takes place. The components involved in the act of interpretation - the interpreter, the text, the context, the code, the culture, the product, etc. - are inextricably intertwined. Furthermore, this subtextual dimension has been embedded into the text because of the interconnection of the text to the Biblical narrative. This constitutes the text's *intertextuality*.

As another example, consider a television commercial for *Miller* beer that was shown regularly during Sunday afternoon football games on American television in the early 1990s. The action of the commercial can be broken down into a sequence of actions as follows:

- As the commercial begins, we see a young man who is seated at a bar counter in a crowded, smoke-filled room, with a beer glass nearby.

- He is surrounded by a group of male companions. They are chatting and confabulating in the ways young men are purported to do in such situations.

- At the other end of the bar, a matched group of males has congregated around another young, handsome "leader of the pack."

- At a certain moment, an attractive female enters the bar scene. Instantaneously, the "leaders" of both male cliques make their way towards her.

- To block the second leader from getting to her first, the first male clique cuts off his path to the female in a strategic manner, leaving the first leader to "get his prize."

- The whole "action" is described by a voice that is reminiscent of a football play-by-play narration.

- Even the ways in which the first male clique carries out its "blocking plan" is described as if it were an action play in a football game.

- The commercial ended with the expression *Love is a game* appearing on the screen.

Given that the commercial was shown - i.e. positioned - during football game telecasts, and given that the actions that took place in the context of a football game, an appropriate subtextual interpretation can easily be formulated. In a nutshell, the actions of the two cliques would seem to constitute a simulation of a football action play between two teams. "Winning" the game in this case is "getting to" the female prize. In order to accomplish this, the first male leader, or "quarterback," needs the support of his "team" to be effectual in carrying out the crucial play, which of course he is. By successfully blocking the path of the other team's quarterback to the girl, the first quarterback wins the "game." He "scores" sexually, as the expression goes.

Interpreting the commercial text in terms of a football game is reinforced by the play-by-play description of an announcer whose voice and descriptive style are made to emulate those of a television football announcer, as well as by the concluding statement that ap-

pears on the screen: *Love is a game*. The subtext is now rather conspicuous. It is enunciated explicitly by this statement. The commercial also alludes to two *intertexts* - namely, the actual game rules of
football and the typical ways in which a TV announcer describes
game plays.

2.2.2 Decoding

The process of uncovering a subtextual meaning in an ad text is
commonly referred to as *decoding*. This is an appropriate term, for it
encapsulates what is involved - namely, the identification of the code
or codes utilized to generate a signification system in the ad.

Generally, the codes are used to deliver metaphorically structured connotative meanings. In the case of the *Marilyn Peach* ad the
subtext is anchored on at least one metaphorical idea - *Sex is a forbidden desire*. But, as we saw, there were several other interpretative
paths that could have been pursued. Indeed, the metaphorical open-
endedness of the subtext gives the ad its psychological richness. The
more literal an ad, the less effective it is at a subtextual level. Note
that what is emphasized in the subtext of the ad is not an actual sexual experience, but the whole notion of sex as a forbidden fruit. The
ad also associates sex metaphorically with the figure of the snake -
which not only connotes Evil but is also a metaphor for the penis.
The subtext thus creates symbolic associations between the product
and what consumers covet, between phallic symbolism and mythical
feelings, etc.

Take, as another example, *Budweiser* beer. *Budweiser* ads speak
to average young males and to the realities of male bonding. This is
why *Bud* ads show males hanging out together, performing bizarre
male bonding rituals, and generally expressing culturally based notions of male sexuality. The subtext in these ads is: *You're one of the
guys, bud*.

The use of several codes in tandem to create the subtext can be
called *intercodality*. Representation in advertising is often carried out
intercodally. through a deliberate use of various codes to create a
signification system for a product. Assigning a name to a product,
with all the connotations that this entails, involves the use of the

naming code of a culture; the creation of logos or trademarks involves the use of the *art code* of a culture; the composition of jingles to impart a recognizable musical identity to the product involves, needless to say, a use of the *musical code* or *codes* of a culture, etc. Intercodality can be represented graphically as follows (figure 3):

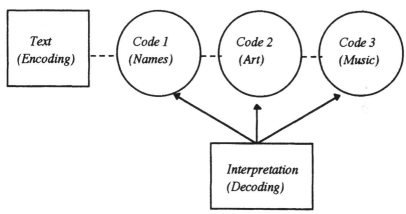

Figure 3. Intercodality

It is to be noted that both the maker of an ad or commercial and the interpreter must have access to the same codes. This simple model shows why semiotic method applied to advertising is characterized as the science of decoding, for it aims to unravel the codes used in making up texts and the connotative meanings that these engender.

Consider, as another example of decoding an ad for *Iron Cologne* that was included in mainstream fashion magazines like *Cosmopolitan*, suggesting a female viewing audience, during the late 1990s. In the ad text, we see the following features:

- There is a handsome, muscular, sensuous man embracing a voluptuous woman dressed up for physical exercise.

- The shade of the ad is bluish, the color of the cologne bottle.

- At the bottom of the page is an insert showing the bottle of perfume being sprayed.

- The insert seems to be "underneath" the main visual text: i.e. the actual ad text has been "ripped" at its bottom right corner to expose the "hidden" cologne bottle.

- The expression *Pump some iron*, completes the textual presentation.

At a denotative level, the message seems quite simply to be: "Enjoy a great sex life, as physically energetic and satisfying as pumping iron, by wearing *Iron Cologne*, or buying it for your male partner." The message is apparently directed to both males and females. "Denotative meaning," writes Hoshino (1987: 46), "involves a product's surface meaning, which mainly implies its technological and functional meaning (practical and substantial meaning) and corresponds to the consumer's physical needs."

Let us now delve a little deeper into the connotative signification system suggested by the text's signifiers. It is at this connotative level where, as Hoshino (1987: 46) also observes, "a product's deep and hidden meaning, which tacitly and vaguely suggests a non-material meaning, corresponds to the consumer's psychological needs." First, the blue shading is not only synchronized with the color of the cologne bottle, but it could also suggest the "shadow of nighttime," an appropriate time during which to enjoy sex. A closer look at the implied action in the ad reveals that the male is holding the female's hair forcibly, coercively, violently. He is looking down at her. Her eyes, on the other hand, are shut, passively, submissively. We do not see where his other hand is (Could it be fondling her?). It would appear, in short, that the man is about to force the woman down into a supine position for sexual intercourse. The implicit violence of his embrace is reinforced by the ripped insert at the bottom of the page. The act of ripping is forceful and passionate. Also, the exposure of the spraying bottle perhaps reveals what is "underneath" the male's violent act of passion. His desire, in masturbatory terms, is indeed that of a "spray" (ejaculation). The bottle is being sprayed, as a matter of fact, in the same direction as the male's penile orientation. The finger on the sprayer is an indexical sign, pointing out the bottle, the source of his sexual satisfaction.

At this point, the verbal component of the text, *Pump some iron*, can be easily connected to the subtext. At the surface textual level, it can be related to the physically invigorating act ensuing from intercourse. *Pumping iron* in fact describes a body-building activity, which is in line with the perception of male sexuality as strong, violent, and dominant. The man's muscular arms reinforce this interpretation. But in terms of the hypothesized subtext it also suggests the nature of male sexuality. Indeed, it is not uncommon to refer to the sex act colloquially as *pumping*, with the *iron* being an obvious metaphor for an erect penis. The iconic configuration of the three words, *Pump some iron*, is also connotatively suggestive. The three words are presented "one on top of the other," which is indicative of the normal supine position for sexual intercourse. And the sounds of the words themselves, when uttered out loud, suggest the kind of grunting that accompanies sexual intercourse.

This analysis of a possible subtext of this ad makes sense only in a cultural context where masculine sexuality is perceived as aggressive and dominating. Violent sex, which is pleasurable presumably to men, is filtered for the female viewer through the blue shading and soft glare of the ad's color.

2.2.3 Mythologizing the product

The *Marilyn Peach* ad reveals, as mentioned several times, the embedding of a specific mythic code into the make-up of the text - namely the one that enfolds all the connotations derived from the Adam and Eve story. This process, as mentioned in chapter I, is commonly referred to as mythologization (1.1.2)

Consider another example of mythic coding - an ad for *Versus* cologne that appeared in magazines in the mid-1990s. The ad was clearly aimed at affluent, young males who could afford to buy an expensive bottle of cologne. The young men in the ad are prototypes of what young (mid-twenties) urban professional males aspire to look like during leisure hours - hours devoted presumably to mate selection and/or sexual fulfillment generally. During the day, the ad seems to be saying, these men wear suits; during recreational time they wear "V-neck" apparel and splash on *Versus*. So, one possible interpretation of the ad's meaning is that *Versus* fits in nicely with the kind of leisure activities that such male types engage in. It is a cologne designed to help them cross over, symbolically, from the work world to the leisure world - worlds that are in opposition. Now, reasoning mythically, one can argue that the former world is suggestive of the realm of Apollo - the god of male beauty and of the fine arts - and the latter the realm of Dionysus - the god of wine, representing the irrational, undisciplined, and orgiastic side of the male psyche. Is *Versus* the olfactory means by which a modern Apollo can become his Dionysian Self?

This mythic interpretation is strengthened by the fact that the V-shape of the men's collars and of the bottle design "points downwards," i.e. down toward the Dionysian underworld of carnality and unending physical pleasure. *Versus* is, in this interpretative framework, a verbal icon about the conflictual nature of male psychology, constantly oscillating between Apollonian and Dionysian extremes.

The use of dark colors in the ad can also be tied to this interpretative line of reasoning. Darkness connotes fear, evil, the unknown. Children are perpetually afraid of the dark; we stay away from dark forests; we talk of "black masses;" we expect our evil personages in movies and in fictional lore to be dressed in black; we sense that forbidden, mysterious, happenings occur at night; etc. The dark tones of the bottle are suggestive that something dark and dangerous, but nevertheless desirous, is about to happen. *Versus* thus would seem to invite the male viewer to "cross over" (across the page) into the dark underworld where his base, primal urges can be released and satisfied. This world casts dark shadows on the men's faces - shadows that cover their eyes, the mirrors of the soul. In the underworld, there is no soul, no spirituality, just carnality and cupidity. The V-shape intaglio of the *Versus* bottle is indicative of an "opening" into this underworld, a crevice that opens up below a Dionysian world of lust and indulgence.

One of the men in the ad wears a leather hat and another a leather motorcycle jacket. Leather is suggestive of a fetishist quality which, as Sebeok (1991: 121) observes, "bridges the gap between touch and smell." This is why scenes and images of sadism and masochism in our culture often involve the wearing of leather. Are these, perhaps, the forbidden sexual pleasures that *Versus* makes possible?

To complete the interpretive picture being drawn, let us consider, once again, the V-shape intaglio of the bottle, of the first letter of *Versus*, and of the men's necklines. The cologne is meant for men to wear. Now, what sexual objective would men have in wearing it? What is the specific target of their desire? The vaginal shape of the bottle and of the neckline configurations appears to answer this question rather bluntly. But, at this point in the hermeneutic line of reasoning undertaken, another interpretive path opens up. One can ask, in fact, whether the object of the men's desire is not the "opposite" of the vagina, as the name *Versus* suggests at a subtextual level? In other words, does the perfume allow the men to descend even further into deeply-hidden homosexual desires? The good looks of the men, with their darkened eyes looking directly into the camera, muscular bodies, and sensuously-protruding lips, leather apparel, together with the absence of women in the ad, is strongly suggestive of this subtext.

Whether or not the two interpretations put forward here are appropriate, the point we wish to make is that both are seemingly possible. The way the ad is laid out and designed creates an entangled web of ambiguous sexual and macabre connotations:

> *darkness of the night = sexuality = forbidden pleasures = hidden homosexual urges = etc.*

There is obviously much more to *Versus* cologne than smell! The *Versus* ad illustrates rather strikingly how powerful visual texts are in creating chains and chains of connotations, each with its own hermeneutic path for the analyst to pursue. In a certain sense, the *Versus* ad is a small "work of art," which has, however, the aesthetically-trivial purpose of enhancing sales of a product. The iconic features of the ad (the suggestive shape of the perfume bottle and of the men's necklines, the effective juxtaposition of the word *Versus* across the page, the dark shadows, etc.), the symbolic connotations that these evoke (e.g. the allusion of the name *Versus* to "oppositional" tendencies), all intertwine thematically to create a subtext with many ramifications.

The word *myth* derives from the Greek *mythos* "word," "speech," "tale of the gods." It can be defined as a metaphorical narrative that seeks to give order and coherence to experiences by relating them to some existential purpose in terms of time (sequentiality), space (location, eventuality), and cause (ascribed to some metaphysical entity, happening, or event). In the primordial stages of human culture, myths were genuine "theories" of the world, aiming to explain it with what the great Italian philosopher Giambattista Vico (1688-1744) called the *poetic imagination.* Mythical narratives continue to form the basis for imparting knowledge of the world to children poetically and imaginatively. There are no cultures without stories, fables, and legends to explain the origins of things, people, morals, values, etc. Narrativity appears to be a fundamental sense-making operation of the mind. It is a common experience that we remember stories more easily and vividly than we do isolated concepts and words.

The narrative structure of the myths of early cultures allows us to reconstruct the *forma mentis* of that people. The crucial thing to note is that those myths have not disappeared from communal memory or social traditions. As psychoanalysis has maintained for years, there seems to be a kind of "mythic unconscious" in humanity that constitutes a powerful shaper of conscious activities. According to some scholars of mythology (e.g. Campbell 1969; Heinberg 1989) our primordial acts of conscious social activity (hunting, gathering, etc.) constitute the source of many mythic themes. As Campbell (1969: 59-60) has observed, these encode fear and awe of the world of Nature itself. During the primitive stages of all societies myth was the primary mode by which cultures come to establish communal sense-making. Not possessing the knowledge to understand or "explain" environmental events logically and rationally, the first humans ascribed them to awesome and frightful "gods" or "divine" creatures, thus producing humanity's first *archetypes* (literally, original models of things). Myths were created to allow the first hominids living in groups to make sense of the world together, and their narrative structure betray the actual metaphorical structure of human cognition. There is no irony, for example, in early myths and cultures. For Vico, irony is the characteristic feature of a highly abstract rationalistic state of mind - the one that develops later, both phylogenetically and ontogenetically.

Barthes (1957) claimed that advertising taps into the mythic level of mind by virtue of the fact that its texts embed mythic themes within them. This is why, he argued, such texts cannot help but have an effect on us subconsciously. Myths allow us to define ourselves as individuals and as groups. Advertisements are, in a certain sense, modern-day myths that satisfy the inbuilt need for myth that humans living in highly materialistic contexts experience: i.e. while modern peoples no longer rely on myths to explain the world, they still require the psychological power of the poetic imagination to "explain" things to them in metaphysical ways. This continues to thrive in different forms - in cultural mythologies, in superstitions, and in the connotative substance of many advertisements.

2.3 Using multiple media

In addition to creating a signification system for a product through brand naming, logo-creation, and textuality, the use of repetition in different media of the same system is, as pointed out at the start of this chapter, a primary strategy used to enhance product recognizability. This is why the two types main types of media - print and electronic - are often used in tandem in the promotion of a product. In radio, television, and many Internet commercials, product textuality is delivered through narrative and dramatic formats, and reinforced by linguistic and musical elements.

2.3.1 Print media

Print ads reach people through *newspapers*, *magazines*, *direct mail*, and *outdoor signs*:

- *Newspapers*, on average, devote almost half of their space to advertising. These offer advertisers several advantages over other media. Most adults read a daily newspaper; and many specifically check the ads for information about products, services, or special sales. Newspaper advertising can also quickly incorporate a sudden demand for certain merchandise.

• *Magazines* have a number of advantages over newspapers. They are usually read in a leisurely manner and are often kept for weeks or months before being discarded. They also offer better printing and color reproduction.

• *Direct mail* advertising includes the use of leaflets, brochures, catalogues, and other printed advertisements that are delivered by a postal service.

• *Outdoor signs* are used because people pass by the signs repeatedly. In addition, large, colorful signs attract attention. The main kinds of outdoor signs include: posters, painted bulletins, illuminated displays, transit signs, window displays, and point-of-purchase displays.

The print medium bolstered by the use of illustrations, color, photography, etc. is a semiotically powerful one. The use of artwork in a variety of forms enhances the sale of a product, service, or idea by virtue of the fact that it embeds its signification system in visual ways. Before the development of printing, most people could not read; therefore, clear images indicated the nature of the services offered. For example, a *pig in effigy* would adorn a pork-butcher's shop. Art in printed matter became commonplace after the Industrial Revolution.

Posters, as we saw in the previous chapter (1.2), constitute the oldest advertising texts known. In the early nineteenth century two events opened the modern era of poster production: large-scale industrialization created a need for extensive advertising, and the invention of lithography, a printing method, made it easier for artists to include colored illustrations on posters. Beginning in 1867, the artist Jules Chéret revolutionized the look of posters, using illustrations as the dominant features while reducing the verbal text to a minor explanatory role. Chéret's methods gave rise to visually charming commercial posters that were understandable even to non-literate people. His techniques continue to be used to this day. In the 1890s several *art nouveau* artists introduced important innovations. These included the use of large areas of flat color and the replacement of the idealized figures of human beings with naturalistic or caricatured figures depicted in telling vignettes. The art nouveau artists also introduced flowing lines and elegant, elongated forms to create exotic, stylized illustrations. Their techniques are being used to this very day.

One of the most effective means of print advertising is known as *direct advertising*. This refers to all forms of sales appeals mailed, delivered, or exhibited directly to the prospective buyer of an advertised product or service, without use of any indirect medium, such as newspapers or television. The chief functions of direct-mail advertising are to familiarize prospective buyers with a product, its name, its maker, and its merits and with the product's local distributors.

Used for the same broad purposes as direct-mail advertising, *unmailed* direct advertising includes all forms of indoor advertising displays and all printed sales appeals distributed from door to door, handed to customers in retail stores, included in packages and bundles of merchandise, or conveyed in some other manner directly to the recipient.

2.3.2 Electronic media

Radio advertising has the advantage that people can listen to programs while doing other things, such as driving a car or working at home. Another advantage is that radio audiences, in general, are more highly selectable by the type of programming than are television audiences. For example, stations that feature country music attract different kinds of listeners than do those that play rock. By selecting the station, advertisers can reach the people most likely to buy their products. Radio commercials include direct sales announcements, dramatized stories, and songs. Most commercials last 30 to 60 seconds.

Television advertising has become the most effective contemporary medium for delivering product image because it brings sight, sound, and action directly to consumers in their homes. Advertisers can explain and demonstrate their products to viewers who are enjoying a TV program and cannot easily avoid the commercials. Network television reaches a vast, nationwide audience at a very low cost per viewer. The majority of TV commercials consist of short spot announcements, most of which last 30 seconds to a minute. The commercials are usually run in groups of three to six. Television networks and stations generally limit commercial time to about 10 minutes per hour during prime time and 16 minutes per hour during most other broadcast times.

Lastly, the Internet has become a highly effective medium of advertising since its advent in the 1990s. The Internet has made it possible for people all over the world to communicate effectively and inexpensively with each other. Unlike traditional broadcasting media, such as radio and television, the Internet is a decentralized system. Each connected individual can communicate with anyone else on the Internet, can publish ideas, and can sell products with a minimum overhead cost. Commercial use of the Internet is growing dramatically as more individuals gain access to it. Virtually any product or service can now be ordered from Internet sites.

The feature of the Internet that makes it special is the fact that the product or service can be ordered directly *from the ad*. Not only does this an ad about, say, a hotel chain reach millions of potential customers through the World Wide Web, but it users can make reservations by computer "on the spot," by clicking the appropriate icons.

Interestingly, in 2001 the carmaker BMW took to the web in great style, showing how this medium may, in fact, have become a critical one for getting the ad message out. BMW hired several famous directors to make short "digital films" featuring its cars. The movies were viewable only on the Web, but were promoted through TV spots. Those digital commercials clearly blurred the line between art and advertising, showing how a continuity had emerged between the larger cultural order and the advertising domain. Each film was about six minutes long; each featured a prominent actor; and each portrayed BMWs used in a reckless, adventure-oriented fashion. As an example of the globalization of ad culture, it bore concrete evidence of the ever-creeping commercialization of virtually everything.

The Internet also holds out possibilities for creating "product chat rooms." In early 2000, *Vogue* and *W* magazines created just such a website, *Style.com*, where people could click on to get the latest gossip about the fashion industry. The site included material from other companies. Although it was a gossip forum, it nevertheless provided further recognizability for companies.

2.4 Ad campaigns

Repetition is built as well into *ad campaigns*. These can be defined as the systematic creation of a series of slightly different ads and commercials based on the same theme, characters, jingles, etc. An ad campaign is comparable to the *theme and variations* form of music - where there is one theme with many variations.

Here are just a handful of examples of famous ad campaigns through the years:

- In 1892, the *Coca-Cola* logo appeared across the country, painted as a mural on walls, displayed on posters and soda fountains where the drink was served, imprinted on widely marketed, common household items (calendars, drinking glasses, etc.).

- In 1904, the *Campbell's Soup* company began its highly successful advertising campaign featuring the rosy-cheeked *Campbell Kids* and the slogan *M'm! M'm! Good!* The campaign is still ongoing as we write.

- In 1970, *McDonald's* launched its highly successful *You deserve a break today* advertising campaign that is still ongoing.

- In 1985, *Nike* signed basketball player Michael Jordan as a spokesman, marking the beginning of a dramatic growth for the company. *Nike* marketed the *Air Jordan* line of basketball shoes and clothes with a series of striking advertising creations (ads and commercials). Those creations, along with the company's *Just Do It* campaign featuring football and baseball star Bo Jackson and motion-picture director Spike Lee, boosted *Nike's* profits considerably. In 1997, *Nike* entered a new period of high-profile product image when company spokesman Tiger Woods became the first African American (and also the first Asian American) to win the Professional Golf Association's Masters golfing tournament.

- In 1991, the American Medical Association criticized *RJR Nabisco* for using a cartoon character named *Joe Camel* in its *Camel* advertising campaign, claiming that the campaign was targeted at children. In 1992, the US Surgeon General asked the company to withdraw its *Joe Camel* ads, and this request was followed by more government appeals in 1993 and 1994. The company responded to public concerns by promoting a campaign that encouraged store merchants and customers to obey the law prohibiting the sale of tobacco products to minors. In 1997, under increasing criticism, the company ended its *Joe Camel* ad campaign

- The growth of the *Gateway 2000* computer company in the 1990s was helped, in large part, by an unusual advertising campaign featuring employees standing in cow pastures. The company also shipped its computers in boxes splattered with black spots like those of Holstein cows, reflecting its Midwestern roots.

- Interestingly, advertisers have been clever in coopting a widespread "anti-advertising" movement by tapping into it, thus neutralizing it. In 1997, for instance, a *Nike* campaign used the slogan *I am not a target, I am an athlete*, and *Sprite* used *Image is nothing*.

Interestingly, even those who complain against the stranglehold that advertising has on the signification systems present in the cultural order, voice their complaints through advertising campaigns.

One of the primary functions of campaigns is to guarantee that the product's personality keep in step with the changing times. *Pepsi* advertising, for example, has always attempted to do so by emphasizing the changing social climate in its campaigns. A "time capsule" of some of its famous campaigns can be drawn to highlight how *Pepsi* has constantly adapted its textuality to be in tune with the times:

- 1898: An American pharmacist, named Caleb Bradham, gives the brand name *Pepsi-Cola* to his carbonated invention.

- 1903: Bradham produced the first ads with a pharmacological subtext to them: *Exhilarating, Invigorating, Aids Digestion.*

- 1906: Ad headlines are changed to: *The Original Pure Food Drink.* This emphasized the fact that the drink was not some chemical concoction, but a "pure" one, as customers started to challenge the nutritional quality of pop drinks.

- 1920: As society became more affluent, *Pepsi* changed its campaign to reflect it as follows: *Drink Pepsi-Cola: It Will Satisfy You.*

- 1939: The Depression years forced *Pepsi* to change its slogan to: *Twice as Much for a Nickel*, a theme introduced cleverly by the cartoon called *Peter & Pete.*

- 1940: Aware of the growing popularity of music on the radio, *Pepsi* is the first advertiser in history to broadcast a jingle called *Nickel, Nickel.* The jingle was so popular that it became a hit on its own.

- 1943: The new slogan *Bigger Drink, Better Taste* was designed to tap into the new affluence of the era.

- 1949: The slogan *Why Take Less When Pepsi's Best?* reflected a concern over the increasing take over of the market share by other soft drink companies.

- 1950: With its *More Bounce to the Ounce, Pepsi* changed its personality to reflect a new emphasis on vigorous lifestyle.

- 1953-1954: With the growing concern over obesity, *Pepsi* assumed a new weight-conscious personality with its campaign positioning its product as *The Light Refreshment* and *Refreshing without Filling*.

- 1958: *Pepsi* juvenilized its personality, tapping into the new "teen market" with: *Be Sociable, Have a Pepsi*.

- 1963: Even more aware of the burgeoning "youth generation" *Pepsi* renamed it outright *The Pepsi Generation*.

- 1966: A jingle called *Girlwatchers*, which is self-explanatory in its emphasis on a growing openness in sexual mores, became a top 40 hit.

- 1967: With its *Taste that Beats the Others Cold: Pepsi Pours it On* campaign, *Pepsi* tapped into a growing competitiveness in society.

- 1969: The hippie movement and its emphasis on giving and helping others was captured with the new slogan: *You've Got a Lot to Live. Pepsi's Got a Lot to Give*.

- 1973: The themes of freedom and youth tribalism that the hippie movement had spawned were encapsulated in *Pepsi's* new *Join the Pepsi People, Feelin' Free* campaign.

- 1975: The growing challenges facing a constantly changing technological society were reflected in *Pepsi's Pepsi Challenge* campaign.

- 1976: With its *Have a Pepsi Day* campaign in which a little boy encounters puppies in commercials was designed to tap into a growing sensitivity to the issues of childhood in society at large.

- 1979-1982: Two campaigns - *Catch the Pepsi Spirit, Drink it In!* and *Pepsi's Got the Taste for Life* - were designed to capture the growing egoism of the times, now characterized as the "Me Generation."

- 1984-1985: *Pepsi* coopted pop culture stars, reflecting the growing power of the media in society and the fact that young people of the era were the first generation to have grown up as "TV's babies." Michael Jackson declared *Pepsi "The Choice of a New Generation,"* and Tina Turner, Gloria Estefan, Lionel Ritchie, Joe Montana, Dan Marino, Teri Garr, and Billy Crystal were featured in *New Generation* commercials on television. Michael J. Fox starred in the classic commercial *Apartment 10G.*

- 1987-1993: The above textuality was extended as *Pepsi*, which in 1987 called itself *America's Choice*, used Michael Jackson as the star of its episodic four-part *Chase* commercial. In 1990 teen stars Fred Savage and Kirk Cameron were featured in commercials entreating their peers to join the *New Generation*, and music legend Ray Charles grooved to the times with *You Got the Right One, Baby, Uh-Huh!* Other celebrities declared *Gotta Have It* and *Been There, Done That, Tried That* on commercial slots, tapping into the growing *ennui* among affluent teenagers of the era. This campaign culminated in 1993 with basketball star Shaquille O'Neal exhorting his viewers to *Be Young, Have Fun.*

- 1995-1997: With its *Nothing Else Is a Pepsi* and *Security Camera* campaigns, the pop drink company showed itself as being unique among the competition, in line with a growing stress on individuality and Self-identity in society. With *GeneratioNext* in which the Spice Girls were featured, *Pepsi* revamped its *Pepsi Generation* theme, with this clever bit of self-reference.

- 1998: *Pepsi's Dancing Bears* campaign, with its humorous tone, taped into a growing emphasis on sitcom-style behavior in social interaction.

- 1999: Tapping again into the power of pop culture stars as the icons of society, *Pepsi's Joy of Cola* campaign featured such classic icons as Marlon Brando, Isaac Hayes, Aretha Franklin, and Jeff Gordon.

- 2002: Aware of the tendency in society to maintain a "youthful" look and lifestyle, no matter what one's age, *Pepsi* introduced its *Forever Young* campaign, emphasizing that *Pepsi* is the drink of everyone who thinks and looks young, no matter what their age.

2.4.1 Cooption

As the above historical chronology clearly shows, the most effective type of campaign seems to be the one that *coopts* social themes. In the 1960s, for example, the image created by the media of self-proclaimed "rebels" and "revolutionaries," referred to generally as "hippies," who genuinely thought they were posing a radical challenge to the ideological values and lifestyle mores of the mainstream consumerist culture, ended up becoming the unwitting trend-setters of the very culture they deplored, providing it with features of lifestyle and discourse that advertisers have, since the 1960s, been able to adapt and recycle into society at large. Counterculture clothing fashion was thus quickly converted into mainstream fashion, counterculture music style into mainstream music style, counterculture symbolism and talk into society-wide symbolism and discourse - hence the crystallization of a social mindset whereby every individual, of every political and ideological persuasion, could feel that he/she was a symbolic participant in the "youth revolution."

The use of the hippie image in ads and commercials of the era occurred at a point in time when a dynamic business community decided it was in its best interest not to fight the images of youth insurgency, but rather to embrace them outright. One highly effective early strategy of this "if-you-can't-beat-them-join-them" approach was the development of an advertising style that mocked consumerism and advertising itself! The strategy worked beyond expectations. Being young and rebellious came to mean having a "cool look;" being anti-establishment and subversive came to mean wearing "hip clothes." The corporate leaders had cleverly "joined the revolution," so to speak, by deploying the slogans and media images of youthful rebellion to market their goods and services. "New" and "different" became the two key words of the new advertising and marketing lexicon, coaxing people into buying goods, not because they necessarily needed them, but simply because they were new, cool, hip. The underlying system of signification of this clever marketing strategy allowed consumers to believe that what they bought transformed them into ersatz revolutionaries without having to pay the social price of true nonconformity and dissent.

Campaigns, such as the *Pepsi Generation* and the *Coke* universal brotherhood ones, directly incorporated the images, rhetoric, and symbolism of the hippie counterculture, thus creating the illusion that the goals of the hippies and of the soft drink manufacturers were one and the same. Rebellion through purchasing became the subliminal thread woven into the pop culture mindset that the marketing strategists were starting to manipulate and control effectively. The *Dodge Rebellion* and *Oldsmobile Youngmobile* campaigns followed the soft drink ones, etching into the nomenclature of products themselves the powerful connotations of hippie rebellion and defiance. Even a sewing company, alas, came forward to urge people on to join its own type of surrogate revolution, hence its slogan *You don't let the establishment make your world; don't let it make your clothes.* In effect, by claiming to "join the revolution," advertising created the real revolution. This is why, since the late 1960s, the worlds of advertising, marketing, and entertainment have become totally intertwined with youth lifestyle movements, both responding and contributing to the rapid fluctuations in social trends and values that such movements entail.

Today, the advertising industry has appropriated "cool images" so completely that it is no longer recognized consciously as a form of lifestyle that emanated from a subversive movement of the young. Sociologically, the end result has been a further obliteration of the crucial emotional difference that traditional cultures have maintained between the social categories of *young* and *old*. This is why nowadays the rhetoric of youth is quickly transformed by advertising textuality into the rhetoric of all; why the fashion trends of the young are recycled and marketed shortly after their invention as the fashion styles of all; and why the fluctuating aesthetics of the youth culture are quickly incorporated into the aesthetics of society at large. Cultural cool has, in effect, become the social norm.

2.4.2 Creating history

Ad campaigns are not only designed to coopt trends and turn them to advantage for the product, they are often intended to create a "history" for a product, thus linking it to a sense of cultural continuity and communal tradition. This is done in part by simply getting the product "out there," so to speak, into the faces of all, not just a target or market segment of people. The *Coke* campaigns, for example, have always been designed to appeal to everyone by the process of putting the *Coke* name and logo on virtually everything - on pens, on fliers, in magazine ads, on television, etc. As a consequence, virtually everyone alive today will recognize *Coke* and have some understanding of its system of signification. This works for products and services that appeal to everyone - automobiles, cosmetics, insurance, food, beverages, pain tablets, etc. It cannot be used for "controversial" products such as cigarettes and alcohol, and for things that do not have a broad appeal (e.g. certain music styles, certain types of books, etc.).

But perhaps the most effective means to enjoin the ad text into history is to create, simply, appealing ads. These catch the attention of everyone through the aesthetic channel and, thus, quickly become integrated into communal consciousness. In a fascinating book, titled *Twenty Ads that Shook the World* (2000), James Twitchell identifies twenty ads and/or ad campaigns that have, in fact, become part of this consciousness, simply because they were designed cleverly and had mass appeal. As Twitchell (2000: 8) puts it, "They got into our bloodstream." The twenty are worth mentioning here, in chronological order:

(1)   P. T. Barnum's ads (1870s)

(2)   Lydia E. Pinkham's *"Vegetable Compound"* (1880s)

(3)   *Pear's Soap* (1888)

(4)   *Pepsodent's "Magic"* campaign (1920s)

(5)   *Listerine's "If you want the truth"* campaign (1924)

(6)   *Queensboro's* use of radio (1920s)

(7)   New Haven Railroad's *"The Kid in Upper 4"* ad (1942)

(8)   *De Beers' "A Diamond Is Forever"* campaign (1948)

(9)   *Hathaway's "Hathaway Man"* campaign (1951)

(10) *Miss Clairol's "Does She or Doesn't She?"* campaign (1955)

(11) *Marlboro* cigarette's *"Marlboro Man"* campaign (1950s)

(12) *Anacin's "Hammer-in-the-Head"* campaign (1950s)

(13) *Volkswagen's "Think Small"* campaign (1962)

(14) *Coca Cola's "Things Go Better with Coke"* campaign (1964)

(15) Linden B. Johnson's campaign for the presidency (1964)

(16) *Revlon's "Charlie"* campaign (1970s-1980s)

(17) *Absolut Vodka's "Larceny"* campaign (1980s)

(18) *Apple's "1984"* commercial (1984)

(19) The advent of the *infomercial* (1995)

(20) *Nike's "Michael Jordan"* campaign (1990s)

Before the advent of brand-based advertising in the twentieth century, the nineteenth-century entrepreneur, showman and circus operator P. T. Barnum (1810-1891) was already using advertising to create systems of signification for products. The Barnum ads of the 1870s introduced expressions such as the following into the lexicon of advertising and, through metaphorical extension, into everyday discourse:

Don't miss this once-in-a-lifetime opportunity!

Limited edition at an unbelievably low price!

All items must go!

Not to be missed!

Barnum's ad style introduced so-called "hype," saturating language with hyperboles and a high level of emotivity. Lydia E. Pinkham's *Vegetable Compound* ad of the 1880s - an ad designed to promote remedies for female uterine infections - was among the first to become integrated with the product label. Its outline of the grandomotherly Pinkham became a kind of "proto-logo" that captured everybody's fancy. As one of the first to adopt a brand name, the *Pear's Soap* company produced a truly captivating ad in 1888, on which the picture of a lonely child is displayed with an accompanying text:

A specialty for improving the complexion and preventing redness, roughness and chapping, recommended by Mrs. Langtry, Madame Patti and obtained 15 international medals as a competition soap.

This became, in effect, an *objet d'art* inviting people to look at it for the pure aesthetic value that it had - portraying the maudlin sentimentality that childhood had in the late Victorian world. The angelic face of the child tapped nicely into its view of children as innocent creatures.

In the 1920s, *Pepsodent* toothpaste put into effect an ad campaign based on the theme stated explicitly in the headline of all its textual versions:

Magic
Lies in pretty teeth
Remove that film.

The ads showed a man and a woman seated at a restaurant - implying, of course, that having clean teeth is a pivotal requirement of successful courtship. This is one of the first ads to make the association between a product and fact of life. Its subtext was, clearly, *Brush your teeth with Pepsodent and, magically, you will improve your sex life*. In effect, it created one of the first signification systems for a product. Society has not been the same ever since.

The introduction of "scare tactics" was initiated by *Listerine's* ad campaign of 1924, which was emblemized by the caption *If you want the truth - go to a child* integrated with a photo of a mother and child, with the child reacting, by her troubled expression, to the mother's bad breath, and the mother shown with her head turned slightly away from the child so that her halitosis could not be projected towards the child. This was followed by other ads emphasizing the "unpopularity" that ensues from bad breath.

The use of radio to promote a product was initiated by the *Queensboro* corporation in the 1920s. Their commercials transformed advertising. With the accompaniment of catchy music, the employment of dialogue and other dramatic devices, radio literally piped in the advertiser's message simultaneously throughout society. Entire radio programs became associated with products; indeed, radio, like the print media, had become, by the end of the decade, dependent for its survival on commercial interests.

New Haven Railroad's *The Kid in Upper 4* ad of 1942 opened the door to "advocacy advertising," i.e. to the strategy of actually drawing the customer's attention away from the product, so that he or she could ignore the negative aspects associated with the product. Advocacy advertising is used by cigarette, chemical, and alcohol companies. The ad shows a young person in an upper berth, awake, and seemingly pondering something; in the berth below him, two young men sleeping can be seen. The text reveals what the person in the upper berth is thinking - he is thinking of *leaving behind the taste of hamburgers* and *the pretty girl who writes so often*. This strategy of shifting people's attention away from the lousy train service of the era worked rather effectively, as train use went up considerably after publication the ad. So powerful was the ad that the "kid" in the visual appeared in *Life, Newsweek, Time*, in an MGM movie short, and as the theme of a popular song. This ad showed clearly the extent to which advertising had become integrated to the network of meanings and activities that constitute modern-day culture.

De Beers' campaign utilizing the catchy phrase *A Diamond Is Forever*, which started in 1948 and is still ongoing, is one of the first to have employed mythologization in the creation of a signification system. The metaphorical association between *love* and *diamonds* reverberates with ritualistic overtones. Evoking ideas associated with the possession of charms or amulets that guarantee everlasting life or love, this campaign digs deeply into the archetypal subconscious. The diamond evokes connotations of valor, eternity, and all the other themes that make up the substance of legend and history.

The decade of the 1950s brought with it the entrenchment of many contemporary advertising practices. In 1951, *Hathaway* shirts were promoted as distinctive brands, entrenching the use of brands as identifiers of lifestyle personalities, once and for all. *Miss Clairol's* highly successful *Does She or Doesn't She?* campaign of 1955, made the use of slogans a basic feature of advertising. *Marlboro* cigarettes creation of a fictitious character, called the *Marlboro Man* in the 1950s, introduced this very practice into advertising, raising such characters into the history of modern-day folklore. Also in the 1950s *Anacin* showed the power of iconicity by creating ads and commercials portraying pain inside the human head as metaphorically comparable to the clanking sound made by a banging hammer or the harrowing sensation produced by an electric charge.

Volkswagen's wildly successful *Think Small* campaign (1962) promoting its beetle model and *Coca Cola's* similarly effective *Things Go Better with Coke* (1964) illustrate the degree to which advertising's connotations have entered the system of everyday life (Danesi 1999). It is not a coincidence that the phraseology of these campaigns have become part of the vocabulary of everyday discourse.

In 1964, aware of the success that advertising reaped for Eisenhower before him, Linden Johnson's campaign team decided to use an ad designed to tap directly into the social outlook of the youth generation of the era. It showed a little girl in separate frames becoming eventually annihilated by an atomic blast. The theme of *We must love each other, or else die* was a powerful one indeed at the time. That campaign showed how advertising could easily coopt social themes and make them its own. The cooption strategy is evident as well in Revlon's *Charlie* ads of the 1970s and 1980s, which tapped into the growing feminist movement of the era. These showed a female dressed in business attire, carrying a briefcase, and, in a clear reversal of roles, touching the derrière of a handsome young man. More recently, a *Candie's* perfume ad shows a female dressed only in bra and panties in a bathroom with the medicine cabinet open. showing two bottles of the perfume and a massive pile of condoms. The model in the ad has a sexual gleam on her face.

Absolut Vodka's ingenious *Larceny* campaign of the 1980s showed how powerful images, *on their own*, without language, can be. The campaign simply showed a lock on a chain that had obviously been broken. The metaphorical discourse that such an ad generates is limited only by the imagination. Simply put, it speaks volumes - *Break loose, Don't get caught,* etc. - metaphorically.

The power of images had, by the 1980s, become saliently obvious. Advertising not only tapped into this power but made it the *koiné* of everyday social communication. The power of the ad as a work of art became obvious with *Apple Computer's* brilliant *1984* commercial, which was shown on January 22, 1984, during the third quarter of Super Bowl XVIII on television. Obviously evocative of George Orwell's *1984*, and directed by Ridley Scott, whose 1982 movie *Blade Runner* became almost instantly a classic of postmodern cinematic art, the commercial won countless advertising awards and was characterized by advertising moguls as "the commercial that outplayed the game." Orwellian and other "1984-ish" themes have found their way into a host of commercial campaigns, including the most recent one by *Zenith*, which shows automatonic, depersonalized human robots walking all in tandem, without eyes, and a little girl who, with bright eyes, sees a new Zenith television set sitting on a column in the midst of this arid, spiritless, totalitarian world. The apparition and her childlike discovery of the apparition instantly humanizes the mindless throng, as their eyes emerge as if by metamorphosis from a cocoon. The social connotations that this ad evokes are self-evident.

The first infomercial appeared in 1995; since then television channels promoting goods and services all day long have become commonplace throughout the modern world. And, lastly, *Nike's* extremely successful *Michael Jordan* campaign of the 1990s established the practice of coopting pop culture figures as part of a "philosophy of life" rather than as human props in a commercial promotional campaign.

It is no exaggeration to say that the history of modern culture is intrinsically interwoven with the history of advertising. In looking back over the last century, it is obvious that the messages of advertisers, their styles of presentation, and the ways in which they have integrated language with imagery synesthetically has become the fabric of modern modes of communication. As McLuhan (1964: 24) aptly put it, advertising has become the "art" of the modern world.

Chapter III
Creating textuality

The real persuaders are our appetites, our fears and above all our vanity.
The skillful propagandist stirs and coaches these internal persuaders.

Eric Hoffer (1902–1983)

3. Introductory remarks

As mentioned in the previous chapter, *textuality* is one of the primary strategies used to enhance product image and recognizability. It inheres in creating a series of ads and/or commercials that deliver the same signifieds (meanings or themes), using similar kinds of techniques (e.g. characters, jingles, etc.). Product textuality is one of the persuasion techniques used by advertisers to promote product and service recognizability.

As we saw as well in the previous chapter, it works on two levels - a *surface* and an *underlying* one. The *surface level* constitutes the depiction or representation itself, utilizing typically a particular kind of style in which ads and commercials have been created. The *State Farm* ads and commercials, for instance, invariably involve situations of family-based need that are purportedly met by the company through the intervention of friendly and neighborly agents who are always *there* (as the company's jingle puts it) in difficult times. The different versions of *State Farm's* ads and commercials are, in effect, surface variations of an *underlying* signification system, known as the *subtext*, structured around meanings that constitute a *connotative chain* as follows:

State Farm = security = safety = family values = friendliness = trust-
worthiness = etc.

This bi-level mode of meaning delivery can be schematized as follows:

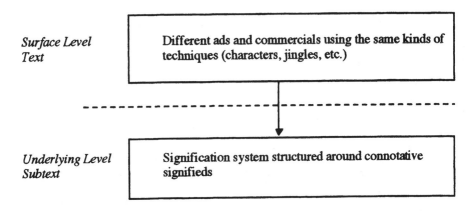

| Surface Level Text | Different ads and commercials using the same kinds of techniques (characters, jingles, etc.) |

| Underlying Level Subtext | Signification system structured around connotative signifieds |

Figure 4.   The surface and underlying levels of ad textuality

The connotations generated by the signification systems created for products are designed to tap into some *buying motive*. Advertisers have identified fifteen main motives (Straubhaar and Larose 2000: 371):

(1) *Achievement:*   the need to achieve meaningful objectives in life;

(2) *Popularity:*   the need to win the attention of others;

(3) *Dominance:*   the need to exert influence in relations;

(4) *Diversion:*   the need to enjoy oneself;

(5) *Understanding:*   the need to teach and instruct;

(6) *Nurturing:*   the need to care for others and be cared for by others;

(7) *Sexuality:*   the need to express sexuality;

(8) *Security:*   the need to be free from harm and threat;

(9) *Independence:*   the need to be self-reliant;

(10) *Recognition:*   the need to be recognized;

(11) *Stimulation:*   the need to have one's senses stimulated;

(12) *Novelty:*   the need to have new things;

(13) *Affiliation:*   the need to win acceptance;

(14) *Support:*   the need to receive support;

(15) *Consistency:*   the need to achieve order.

Given its obvious importance in advertising and marketing, the topic of textuality will be given separate treatment in this chapter. We will start off by decoding a typical print ad in order to illustrate concretely how the surface and underlying levels interact dynamically in the generation of signification systems. Then, we will discuss the connotative structure of subtexts and, lastly, the basic techniques, verbal and nonverbal, that are used in the construction of subtexts.

3.1 Textuality

Recall from the previous chapter the *Versus* ad by *Versace*, which was taken from a lifestyle magazine published several years ago (2.2.3). As mentioned, in the actual *surface text*, the ad spotlights four rugged, handsome young men who presumably wear *Versus* to smell as good as they look. At this surface level, the ad seems to be merely saying: "To look as *cool* as these men, all you have to do is splash on *Versus*." But as our decoding of the ad revealed, the subtext was imbued with many subtle, symbolic innuendoes and allusions that transformed it into a highly suggestive subtext. This was accomplished by a combination of techniques, including *layout, design*, and the generation of *ambiguity*.

3.1.1 Layout and design

To start off, let us consider the ad's most conspicuous iconic cues in terms of its *layout*:

- The name of the cologne starts with the letter "V".

- The bottle displays a V-shaped intaglio in its shape.

- The men in the ad wear either a shirt or jacket whose open collar makes a V-shape outline.

- The men are dressed in black.

- One of the men wears leather.

- The bottle is centered at the bottom.

- The V-shape cuts across the page.

At the surface level, this perfusion of V's strengthens the syntagmatic association between the cologne's name, *Versus*, and its manufacturer, *Versace*. But, as we saw, *Versus* is also a word that connotes "opposition" and "violation," and the V-shape is a symbolic logo that connotes "indentation," "cleft," "fissure." This chain of connotations is reinforced by the fact that the word *Versus* crosses the entire ad, as if it were a line of separation between the men in the ad and the viewers of the ad. The layout, therefore, highlights a set of potential oppositions that the cologne embodies.

Moreover, the layout suggests a kind of "daily story." The ad is clearly aimed at affluent, young males who can afford to buy an expensive bottle of cologne. As mentioned previously, the men are, presumably, prototypes of what young urban professional males aspired to look like during leisure hours several years ago (when the ad was designed) - hours devoted to mate selection and/or sexual fulfillment generally. During the day, the men probably wear business suits; during recreational hours they wear "V-neck" apparel and dash on *Versus*. So, one possible interpretation of the ad's underlying subtext is that *Versus* can be used to aid men in their "sex-seeking" leisure activities. It is cologne designed to help them cross over, symbolically, from the work world to the leisure world - worlds that are in constant opposition. Reasoning mythically, we argued that the former world was the realm of Apollo - the god of male beauty, the fine arts, and order - and the latter the realm of Dionysus - the god of wine, the irrational, and the orgiastic. One interpretation of the *Versus* subtext, therefore, is the following:

The cologne is the olfactory means by which a modern-day Apollo can cross over into the erotically enticing Dionysian realm.

This mythic interpretation is strengthened by the fact that the V-shape of the men's collars and of the bottle design "point downwards," i.e. down indexically to the Dionysian underworld of carnality and sexual pleasure. The dark tones of the clothing and the bottle reinforce this mythic signified, suggesting that something dark and dangerous, but nevertheless desirous, is about to happen. *Versus* thus would seem to invite the male viewer to "cross over" into the dark underworld of sex where he can satisfy his "carnal nature." This world casts dark shadows on the men's faces - shadows that cover the eyes, the mirrors of the soul - for in the underworld, there is no soul, no spirituality, just carnality and ravenous cupidity.

The V-shape intaglio of *Versus* hints at a crevice that is about to open up below a Dionysian world of lust and indulgence. One of the men in the ad wears a leather hat and another a leather motorcycle jacket, both of which are synesthetically suggestive of sado-masochistic eroticism. To complete the interpretive picture being drawn, is the perfusion of V-shapes in the ad. The vaginal shape of the bottle, of the letter "V," and of the neckline configurations are all suggestive of female sexuality.

The signifieds associated with each of the two connotative chains - one suggesting heterosexual indulgence and the other hidden homosexual gratification - can be summarized in chart form as follows:

Table 4. Possible sets of signifieds associated with a *Versus* ad

One set of signifieds (heterosexuality)	Another set of signifieds (homosexuality)
fissure	opposition
cleft	difference
spread	division
opening	cross-over
vagina starts with *v*	The name of the late Versace, a declared homosexual, starts with V

Incidentally, the *design* of the bottle with a V intaglio is a crucial part of the creation of a signification system for the product. As Hine (1995) has amply shown, such things as bottle designs are, in effect, to be viewed as *objets d'art*, as miniature sculptures embedding the meanings that are to be textualized in advertising. Along with the brand name and logo, therefore, the design and/or packaging characteristics of the product are part and parcel components of the process of creating a *personality* or an appeal for the product. Some of these have even been used as true art objects by the *pop art* movement. One of the most famous was produced by Andy Warhol (1928-1987), the American pop artist who made paintings and silk-screen prints of commonplace objects, people, events, etc., such as soup cans and photographs of celebrities. His painting of a *Campbell's* soup can (1964) showed dramatically how powerful product imagery had become in the consciousness of society.

When asked *what* his painting means, people will either: (1) say that it means nothing; or (2) give responses such as "It is a symbol of our consumer society;" "It represents the banality and triviality of contemporary life;" etc. The latter pattern of responses suggests that we typically tend to interpret human-made artifacts as "works of art" because meanings and values are attributed to them by those who make them, by the society in which they live, and by those who look at them in later years. Incidentally, the design of the *Campbell's* soup can underwent a major change in 1994. At the bottom of the red-and-white can there is now a picture of the soup to be found within the container. This has, *ipso facto,* created a new signification system for the product which, before this change, was losing customer loyalty and was thus in need, literally, of a "face lift."

Bottle design is a large part of the fascination of perfume and cologne. For instance, the design for *Houbigant* perfume bottles is cubist, for *Chanel* it is timeless, and for *Minotaur* primordial. *Coke* is recognizable by its bottle as distinct from *Pepsi* or some other soft drink, giving it a feel of something sturdy and classic. The creation of a product personality is, clearly, dependent upon creating meanings, not only through the use of names and logos, but also through bottle or package design.

Aware of the power of design in capturing the aesthetics of the eye, the makers of *Salem* cigarettes attempted in the late 1990s to win over more young smokers by creating a trendier image for its cigarette brand while at the same time attempting to avoid the backlash from society that has beset the cigarette manufacturers in the last decade. Using abstract imagery, akin to that used by symbolist or expressionist painters, *Salem* market tested its new-look product with an ingenious campaign. It mailed out a series of four gift packages -

a box of peppermint tea, a container of Chinese fortune cookies, a bottle of mint-scented massage gel, and finally a candle. Each package - on which a small notice contained the message *Mailing restricted to smokers 21 years of age or older* - came with a coupon for a free pack of cigarettes. The design on each package was highly symbolic and alluring, in line with the occult or mystical signification system that characterizes such things as tea, cookies, and candles. Clearly, the presence of this "New Age" strain in youth culture was something that *Salem* attempted to tap into. *Salem* also changed its "S" logo and package typeface to reflect a more futuristic look, very much in synch with the mystical signification system it has obviously attempted to construct.

One of the more interesting bottle designs can be seen in a recent ad by *Absolut Vodka* - which has the headline *Absolute Ritts*. This shows a picture of the vodka bottle with the silhouette of a nude female body inside it. The name Ritts refers to the photographer Herb Ritts, and the bottle design emulates his own photographs, which are marked by a high degree of sensuality. But this sensuality is tempered by the cool blue background of the sky against which the bottle is cast, creating a sensory opposition and, hence, tension in the viewer. Like the *Versus* ad, it is this oppositional quality that generates a high degree of connotation. Together, the ad and bottle design, like a Ritts photograph, constitute indeed a small work of art.

3.1.2 Ambiguity

As we also saw in the previous chapter, the suggestive power of the *Versus* ad lies primarily in its inbuilt *ambiguity*, i.e. in its ability to generate various kinds of subtexts from the same layout. Building ambiguity into a product, into its brand name, into its logo design, or into its overall textuality is a typical advertising technique. The "homosexual" interpretation of the ad is due in large part to the visual features of the ad. The good looks of the men, their darkened eyes looking directly into the camera, their muscular bodies and sensuously-protruding lips, the leather apparel they are wearing, and the conspicuous absence of women in the ad, are all strongly suggestive of this interpretation.

There are, in fact, other interpretations of the ad, as several sub-jects who viewed it upon our request emphasized to us (mainly students at the University of Toronto enrolled in a first-year semiotics class). Whether or not the two interpretations put forward here are legitimate is, actually, beside the point. The fact that both are possible, as are others, is what imparts a high *connotative index* to the product's textuality. It is this ambiguous textuality, created by the high connotative index, that can be used again and again in the creation of other ads and commercials for the same product.

In effect, the more ambiguous an ad's textuality, the more likely will it create great interest and generate appeal. Needless to say, this is true of any text, brand name, logo, etc. The more interpretations there are, the more the product can be shielded from having its signification system "unmasked." Because the various connotative meanings generated by the subtext are interconnected to the other networks of meanings that are present in a culture, the ad's signification system is, *ipso facto*, intertextual, linking its viewer to this network and thus, surreptitiously imparting a sense of communal meaningfulness in the process.

Consider the *Playboy* logo of a bunny wearing a bow-tie. This is a highly ambiguous design that opens up at least two chains of connotations:

rabbit = female = highly fertile = sexually active = promiscuous = etc.

bow tie = elegance = night club = finesse = richness = Humphrey Bogart = etc.

The appeal and staying power of this logo is due, in our view, to its inbuilt ambiguity, which guarantees that a definitive, singular meaning can never be successfully extracted from it.

3.2 Connotation

Examples such as the *Versus* ad and the *Playboy* logo lead to the conclusion reached by Barthes nearly a half century ago - namely, that from a semiotic standpoint it can be said that advertising is "the art and science of connotation." Thus, in a basic sense, the semiotic study of advertising is a study of connotation.

As we have seen, connotation results from several cognitive processes:

(1) *similarity* (e.g. a V-shape and a cleft);

(2) *difference* (e.g. the same V-shape and its opposite meaning);

(3) *contiguity* (e.g. the location of the V-shape figure *below* the men in the ad);

(4) *intensity* (by highlighting the dark colors in the ad);

(5) *association* (e.g. V-shapes are associated with female genitalia or with crossing over from one place to another).

These often work in tandem in the generation of connotative chains. Suffice it to say that, from a psychological standpoint, the human mind seems predisposed to link meanings together in some way that has its own culture-specific logic. As Goldman and Papson (1996:24) aptly put it, advertising is, in effect, an activity "in which the raw material worked into commodities is *meaning.*" The linkage of meanings is thus effectuve because it unites connotative signifieds in a holistic fashion, making ads and commercial reverberate with implicit sense.

3.2.1 Connotative chains

The two interpretations offered for understanding the appeal of the *Versus* ad were derived from establishing two *connotative chains* suggested by the ad's visual signifiers. Needless to say, other interpretations of the ad's subtext are possible, given the ambiguous nature of the signifiers used in the ad text itself. Indeed, the power of the ad is that it is so ambiguous that it is bound to elicit all kinds of interpretations on the part of viewers, depending on their various experiences with the symbolism employed.

The two chains discussed above can be represented as follows (figure 5):

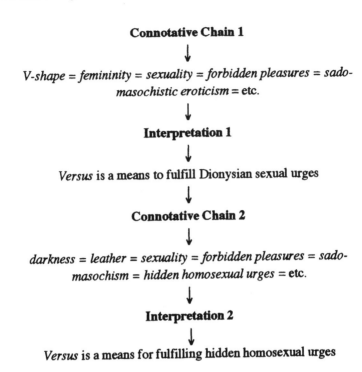

Figure 5. Connotative chains associated with the *Versus* ad

These chains constitute the underlying level of the ad's textuality. The more chains there are, the more suggestive the meanings assigned to the product. In the same time period, other ads for *Versus* showed, in fact, similar surface presentations that appeared to deliver the same kinds of *connotative* meanings in the underlying system of subtextual meanings.

There are various kinds of connotative chains that characterize subtexts. The most common is the one that is forged from *narrative* sources; i.e. it constitutes a chain of meanings linked together by themes, plot-lines, characters, and settings suggested from the implicit storylines built into the surface presentations. The surface text of the *Versus* ad unfolds, as mentioned, as a storyline about male camaraderie and the lifestyle associated with being an upwardly mobile male in today's society; but its subtext was, as we saw, a mythic narrative text. This was created by the many intertextual allusions to the mythic story of Apollo and Dionysus.

Following are brief commentaries on some cases-in-point of magazine ads and ad campaigns that generate narrative subtexts. They were found in various popular lifestyle magazines of the late 1990s:

- An ad by *Dooney & Burke* for a line of their leather tote bags showed a red bag over a puddle of water. The whole scene can be seen to evoke the myth of Narcissus, a beautiful youth beloved by the wood nymph Echo, who refuses her and anyone else who pursues him amorously. The goddess of vengeance, Nemesis, causes Narcissus to fall in love with his own reflection in a pond. Narcissus becomes disembodied, dissolving into the water image of himself on the pond's surface until nothing is left of him but a flower bearing his name. This ad was clearly designed to suggest that the owner of the purse can, like Narcissus, become as elegant and as beautiful as the purse, in this clever retelling of the Narcissus story.

- In an ad for *Rémy Martin* cognac, an attractive female model is shown staring seductively at someone or something beyond the visual perimeter of the ad text. She is holding a lit cigar. The whole ad is in black-and-white, but the smoke billowing from the cigar is cognac-colored, matching the color of the bottle and two glasses containing the cognac on the bottom part of the ad. The logo of the *Rémy Martin* company is that of a satyr, which in Greek mythology was a minor woodland deity, attendant on Bacchus, and usually represented as having pointed ears, short horns, the head and body of a man, and the legs of a goat, and as being fond of riotous merriment and lechery. The female suggests a modern-day embodiment of a satyr - a subtext reinforced by the fact that her bottom half is not shown. A satyr was half human in the top part of its body, and half animal in the lower part. Her glance is clearly indicative of mischief, slyness, artfulness, and lustfulness

all at once - all satyr traits. Her satyr look is further reinforced by the fact that she has pointed ears - another
unmistakable feature of the satyr. The implications that
this mythic narrative has for imbibing *Rémy Martin* are
self-explanatory.

- An ad by *FTD Florist* shows a beautiful young lady
  lying down on a bed and looking directly into the camera with her left arm embracing a vase full of flowers,
  which she obviously has just received as a gift. Her
  look is a blend of satisfaction and insouciance. The
  headline reads: *Heroes always get the girl.* The textuality of this ad is, clearly, reflective of *FTD's* Hermes
  logo - the son of Zeus, who was his father's *heroic*
  messenger and an embodiment of extreme mobility.
  Hermes is also the god of cunning - as reflected in the
  satisfied gleam conveyed by the model's glance.

- A *Givenchy* ad for its product line of *Organza Indé-
  cence* perfume shows a nymph-like model shielding her
  left breast from view. The breast had popped out from
  her low-cut dress, as one of the shoulders is shown as
  being below the shoulder. An arid, dark-green colored
  landscape and sky completes the visual scenery. The
  bottle is shown to the side and just below the covered
  breast with the following caption: *The indecently sensual new fragrance.* The design of the bottle is iconi-
  cally suggestive of the statues of Aphrodite that were
  sculpted in the ancient world. Aphrodite was the goddess of love and beauty. The statuesque quality of the
  human model in the ad is highly synchronized with this
  theme. She appears to be a modern day Aphrodite staring into the camera but with a "far out" look, suggesting eternity.

- The myth of Apollo and Daphne is embedded into an ad
  by *Genny Boutique*. In the black-and-white surface text
  we see a female model wearing *Genny* clothes, staring
  with anticipation at someone beyond the perimeter of

the ad. She is in a dark forest filled with trees in the background. In the original myth Daphne was an ingenuous nymph who was changed into a laurel tree to escape Apollo's advances. The model's look is indeed innocent and nymph-like. Like Daphne she seems to be on the verge of blending into the background and, thus, of becoming a tree.

* And, finally, an ad for *Prada* clothes shows a fierce looking, yet highly enticing, young model lying down on a rock formation between two cliffs in a gorge that is filled with vapor. The model's legs are slight open in an obviously inviting sexual manner. The power of female sexuality and its interconnectedness with Nature is clearly emphasized in this ad. The mythic tale that it evokes is that of Gaia, the goddess who was the personification of the earth, the mother of the Titans. Her earthiness and blatant sexuality was in contrast to the ingenuousness and naiveté of Daphne.

The ways in which these truly remarkable visual "artworks" deliver their subtexts is through mythic narrativity. Their power lies in evoking the connotative chains that myths invariably generate.

Another strategy for engendering connotative chains is, as we have seen in the case of the *Versus* ad, is to utilize oppositions. Consider a recent ad by *Calvin Klein* for its *Contradiction for Men* line of cologne:

* it shows a black-and-white photo of a young man;

* he dressed in a leather jacket;

* he can be seen lovingly embracing and kissing a naked male child;

* the child seems satisfied and happy;

* he also can be seen wearing a silver or steel watch rather conspicuously;

- the bottle - an *objet d'art* resembling a modern mono-
lithic sculpture - is placed in the right hand corner, and
is the only signifier that is in color (the color is silvery
and thus does not really stand out).

There are many "contradictions" indeed in this ad. First, there is
the obvious one of the man assuming the traditional role assigned to
females - caring lovingly for the baby, and thus showing his feelings
overtly. But there is also an oppositional meaning - Nature vs. Culture - as suggested by the fact that the baby is naked (a natural state)
but the man clothed in a leather jacket (a cultural state). Then there is
a synesthetic opposition induced by the feeling of leather touching
naked skin. Another synesthetic effect is created by the fact that the
man is wearing a watch made of silver or steel. Other oppositions
include the fact that the man is strong but tender, caring yet manly.
This play on oppositional features produces endless chains of connotations that greatly enhance the *connotative index* of the ad.

3.2.2 The connotative index

Whether or not the subtexts embedded in the *Versus* and *Calvin
Klein* ads will induce consumers to buy their colognes is open to
question. As mentioned in the opening chapter, it is certainly not the
goal semiotics to determine this. The point of the above analysis has
been simply to illustrate that the key to unlocking a product's signification system is to consider the signifiers used to represent it in ads
in a sequence, just like a comic strip, in order to see where the sequence leads in the underlying level.

Now, research conducted by the authors of the present manual
on product imagery has suggested to us that the more interpretations
there are - i.e. the more connotative chains brand names, logos, bottle
designs, magazine ads, TV commercials, etc. generate in different
individuals - the more likely is the product to appeal to subjects. This
suggests a general principle as follows (Beasley, Danesi, and Perron
2000: 57):

The higher the number of connotative chains generated, the greater is the likelihood that the product will appeal to consumers.

The relative number of chains - *high, average, low* - that a product's name, logo, textuality, etc. tends to produce can be called its *connotative index*. Informal studies conducted by the authors of this manual several years ago have suggested that this is a valid notion. In one study, 10 subjects were given ads determined beforehand to have relatively *high, average*, and *low connotative indexes* through textual analyses such as the ones conducted above. The subjects were asked simply to identify which of the ads they thought produced the most thoughts and meanings in their minds.

There were 30 ads in all, 10 rated beforehand as having a *high index*, 10 as having an *average index*, and 10 as having a *low index*. The 10 with the *high index rating* (mainly perfume/cologne ads) were, in fact, identified by all 10 subjects as being highly suggestive and appealing. Some of these produced over 12 different interpretations (connotative chains). The subjects rated the remaining 20 ads as less suggestive, of which they considered 8 to be relatively more suggestive (= *average index*). These were ads for home products and services (insurance, detergents, etc.) that were also rated beforehand as having *average indexes*. The remaining 12 were identified as being the least suggestive by the subjects. Of these, only 2 were rated beforehand as having *average indexes*; the others were, in fact, also pre-rated as having *low indexes*. The latter were all taken from trade magazines announcing products and services in a straightforward "classified ad" manner, although pictures and various symbols were nevertheless used.

The above informal experiment was repeated several times with different subjects using different kinds of ads. Similar results were recorded each time. Clearly, not all advertisements are designed to generate high connotative indexes. Classified ads, which are normally laid out simply to relay information about some product or service, can be said to have a 0 connotative index. On the other hand, the index can be said to be at a maximum in ads and commercials that promote the use of products associated with some aspect of lifestyle (perfumes, clothes, cigarettes, alcohol, automobiles, etc.). The index of every other type of ad or commercial falls somewhere in between these two extremes. The index can be thus conceived to be a continuum, with 0 connotation (pure denotative or informational content) at one end and a maximum connotation point (open-ended, ambivalent, ambiguous content) at the other. Classified ads, ads in trade manuals, and the like tend to fall in the sector of the continuum nearest to the denotative end-point, whereas lifestyle ads tend to fall in the sector that becomes progressively more connotative (figure 6):

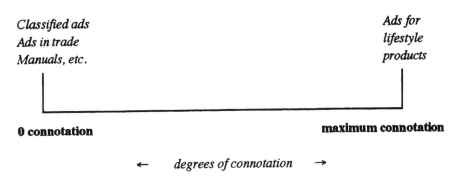

Figure 6. The connotative continuum

The concept of connotative index has been derived, in part, from Barthes' (1977) notion of anchorage (2.2.1). Anchorage implies that ad texts with a high index are constructed in such a way that they can generate connotations from which the viewer can choose some and ignore others: i.e. the text's underlying connotative (associative) structure is anchored to specific meaning domains by different interpreters.

3.2.3 Intertextuality

The fact that an ad may suggest more than one subtext is, as mentioned several times, due to *intertextuality* (2.2.1). Intertextuality is, in a phrase, the co-presence of other texts in the ad. Intertextuality links the ad to the meaning networks in a culture. This means that a subtext can only be deciphered meaningfully (if at all) in specific cultural contexts. The connotations of darkness, oppositeness, etc.

extracted from the *Versus* ad above would hardly be interpreted in Dionysian terms by people living in cultures where the Apollo/Dionysus myth does not exist. In other words, the decoding of subtextual meanings will vary not only according to the analyst's whims, but also the specific culture in which the decoding takes place.

As the analyses of the *Versus* and *Marilyn Peach* ads have revealed, mythic subtexts are very powerful because they are archetypal. The themes of the first myths have not disappeared from modern cultures; they continue to work at an unconscious level. As Roland Barthes (1957) cleverly demonstrated, in early Hollywood westerns, for instance, the mythic "good" vs. "evil" theme was symbolized by heroes wearing white and villains black hats. Sports events, too, are perceived symbolically as mythic battles between "good" (the home team) and "evil" (the visiting team). The whole fanfare associated with preparing for the *World Series* of baseball or the *Superbowl* of American football, has a ritualistic quality to it that invokes the same kind of pomp and circumstance that ancient mythic armies engaged in before going out to battle and war. The symbolism of the home team's (= army) uniform, the valor and strength of star players (= the heroic warriors), and the strategic and tactical capacities of the coach (= the army general) stir the emotions of the fans (= the warring nation). The game (= the battle) is thus perceived to unfold in mythic terms.

Consider the high heel shoes example one more time (1.2.3). At a biological level, *shoes* have a very important function indeed - they enhance locomotion considerably. They are, at this denotative level, artificial locomotion-enhancing "extensions" of the human foot. But, as we saw, in social settings, shoes invariably take on a whole range of connotations. Up till the eighteenth century "shoe fashion" was the privilege of the aristocracy. The Industrial Revolution made possible the manufacture of fashionable clothes and footwear for the common person, making shoe fashion for the masses an economic possibility. Today, fashion trends and styles are dictated by media personalities, fashion moguls, and other high profile personages. High heel shoes in today's society invariably are perceived as sexual props. The broad range of sexual connotations associated with wearing high heel shoes are embedded directly into high heel shoe brands. To the outsider, the manifestations of sexual dressing may look arbitrary - after all, high heel shoes are rather uncomfortable (especially if the heel is high and thin). That's because sexual style is selective in a way that reveals itself. But to the individual living in a modern culture, they resonate as powerful symbols of sexuality.

3.3 Verbal techniques

The surface text of the *Versus* ad was relatively "silent" ones, in the sense that the only meaningful words in it was the brand name itself. As we saw, however, the text nevertheless tells a story. But language is, more often than not, an important contributor to establishing the connotative structure of product imagery. The use of verbal techniques to create effective advertisements and commercials for instance - ads with attention-getting headlines, with slogans designed to help create a favorable image of a company and its products, etc. - is a fundamental part of product textuality.

Consider the *Iron Cologne* ad again (2.2.2). As we saw, at the surface level, the ad shows the following things:

- There is a handsome, muscular, sensuous man embracing a voluptuous woman.

- The shade of the ad text is bluish, the same color of the cologne bottle.

- At the bottom of the page is an insert showing the bottle of cologne being sprayed.

- The bottle is underneath the main visual text, as implied by the fact that the ad text itself is shown as having been "ripped" at its bottom right corner to expose the "hidden" cologne bottle.

- The expression *Pump some iron*, completes the text.

The blue shading is not only in synch with the color of the cologne bottle, but it also suggests the "shadow of nighttime," an appropriate time period during which to carry out sexual activities. The male can be seen to be pulling the female's hair forcibly. He is looking down at her. Her eyes, on the other hand, are shut submissively. The implicit aggressiveness of the man's embrace is reinforced by the ripped insert at the bottom of the page. The act of ripping is forceful and passionate. And, finally, the exposure of the spraying bottle reveals what is really "underneath" the male's act of passion. His desire, in masturbatory terms, is indeed fulfilled in the form of a "spray." As we also saw, reinforcing this interpretation is the fact that the bottle is being sprayed in the same direction as the male's penile orientation. At a literal level the expression *Pump some iron* suggests that the strenuous activity associated with lifting weights will lead to a more robust romantic life. But at a metaphorical level it suggests something else that is more congruous with the ad's underlying meaning - *pumping* is in fact a metaphor for male masturbation and *iron* for the penis.

3.3.1 Figurative language

The use of figurative language is a basic verbal technique for generating product textuality. Consider two other ads as illustrative cases-in-point - one for the perfume *Volupté* and the other for *L'Effleur* fragrance products, both of which appeared in magazines several years ago. *Volupté* is designed to appeal to women in their twenties and thirties:

- The first thing to note is that the perfume's name means "voluptuousness" in French.

- The bottle is placed in the center of the text. It has a dark, round bottle cap.

- The phrase *Trust your senses* is placed just below the perfume bottle; this implies, at a literal level, that the buyer will be able smell the high quality of the perfume.

The shape of the perfume bottle leads directly to the subtext. The bottle cap in particular is highly suggestive of an aroused nipple - a sign of successful sexual foreplay. The phrase *Trust your senses* is, in tandem with this image, suggestive of sexual "sensing," since a breast involves most of the senses in foreplay - sight, smell, taste, and touch. The background scene in the ad reinforces this interpretation, since it shows a secluded, dark place where the bottle (= female breast?) can be looked at voyeuristically through the beam of light that falls upon it.

In contrast, the *L'Effleur* ad spotlights flowers in the shape of a heart, emphasizing pure romantic love. The theme of romance and sweet infatuation is reinforced by a woman's white dress, by the hug given to her by a little girl (a sign of innocent affection), and by the butterflies and angels embedded in the floral arrangement shown. In a phrase, the ad draws a picture of love as idyllic, bucolic, sentimental - a picture reinforced metaphorically by the little love poem included at the bottom:

First Love
Befitting and fragrant
we send bouquets
to the one who gave us yesterdays.

Recall the *Miller* beer commercial described in the previous chapter (2.2.1). One of the features of that commercial was the fact that it ended with the metaphorical expression, *Love is a game*, appearing on the screen. This expression is, in fact, highly reflective of one of the ways in which love is conceptualized in Western culture. We seem to perceive love and mating rituals as "games" to be played out according to specific rules. The statement reflects, in other words, one of the ways in which we think about love, as the following common examples of discourse reveal:

- She left him, because de didn't *play* by the rules.

- He *lost* her to his best friend.

- She attempted to *win* his affections, but didn't.

- He didn't quite *score* with her the other night.

- Their love has lasted because they have always *played* on a even field.

The Miller beer commercial clearly tapped into this conceptual realm, structuring its entire textuality around it. The actual statement of the metaphorical formula at the end of the commercial is, in effect, a verbal index pointing directly to this realm.

Many brand names are metaphors (Wolfe 1989). For example, the perfume named *Poison*, by *Christian Dior*, has an immediate impact because "the apparent contradiction between product description or denotation - a lethal substance - and connotation - a seductive one" that evokes "mystery, alchemy and the archetype of the sorceress" (Wolfe 1989: 3). The meanings that emerge from the metaphor are themselves connotative chains. Take, as an example, the perfume named *Poison*. The meaning of *poison* that the product name is designed to convey is, needless to say, not its denotative one, but rather, the culture-specific connotations perceived in poison - namely, as something harmful or destructive to happiness or welfare. In this way, one can *poison the mind, poison the soul, poison one's life,* etc.

Brand names of lifestyle products, as Dyer (1982: 141) remarks, certainly do more than just identify the product. Through metaphor, they convey arrays of connotative meanings:

> The names given to cosmetics and other beauty products frequently recall images of beauty, cleanliness, sophistication and naturalness: *Moondrops, Natural Wonder, Rainflower, Sunsilk, Skin Dew.* Sometimes the names of products convey scientific authority: *Eterna 27, Clinique, Endocil, Equalia.* Men's toiletries (not "beauty products," you notice) also have evocative names: *Brut, Cossak, Denim, Aramis, Devin.* And it doesn't take much imagination to work out why cigarette brands are called by such names as *Piccadilly, Embassy, Sovereign, Consulate, State Express, Lambert and Butler,* nor why there are cars called *Jaguar, Mustang, Triumph, Princess.*

Lakoff and Johnson (1980, 1999) assert that a large portion of cultural groupthink is built on such metaphorical images, which they call *cultural* or *cognitive models*. Before Lakoff and Johnson's trendsetting work, the study of metaphor fell within the field of *rhetoric*, where it was viewed as one of various *tropes* - i.e. figures of speech. But since the mid-1950s the practice has been to use the term *metaphor* to refer to the study of all figurative language and to consider the other tropes as particular kinds of metaphor. Within this framework, *personification*, for instance (*My cat speaks Chinese*), would be seen as a particular kind of metaphor, one in which the target domain is an animal or inanimate object and the source domain a set of vehicles that are normally associated with human beings.

Metaphor is one of the operative strategies in the creation of a brand identity. Take, for example, automobiles. The names assigned to cars are typically metaphorical, thus enhancing the association between the car itself and some lifestyle pattern or other social and individual meanings embedded in the signification system created for the car. Here are some examples:

Names designating forward movement, achievement, exploration:

Excel
Maxima
Jetta
Explorer
Pathfinder
Achieva
Probe
Landrover
Rangerover

Names designating animals (and thus all the social connotations ascribed to the animals):

Beetle	(= small and quick)
Taurus	(= bullish, tough, and strong)
Colt	(= fast)
Mustang	(= very fast)
Cougar	(= the fastest and most powerful)

Pony	(= young, small, has potential for speed)
Rabbit	(= cute and small)
Ram	(= strong and tough)

Names indicating that the car is a friend, helper, etc.:

Protégé
Sidekick
Escort

Names indicating what the car can be best used for in line with individual lifestyle preferences:

Outback
Towncar
Seville
New Yorker
Metro
Villager
Bonneville
Daytona
Riviera

Names with artistic connotations and, thus, classic qualities:

Sonata
Stanza
Tempo
Prelude

Foreign names that impart exotic and chic connotations to ownership of the car:

Cavalier
LeSabre
Le Baron
Le Car

Grand Prix
Bonneville
Corsica

Names referring to Nature and thus creating a feeling of freedom, back-to-Nature, and even tribal-mythical primordiality:

Windstar
Aerostar
Breeze
Sunfire
Firebird
Sundance

Although interest in metaphor was kindled a long time ago by Aristotle (384-322 BC), the scientific study of its relation to cognition and communication is a relatively recent phenomenon. Aristotle was, in fact, the one who coined the term *metaphor* - itself a metaphor (*meta* "beyond" + *pherein* "to carry"), because he noticed that this form of language revealed how we produce knowledge. The sapient animal was a metaphorical thinker, Aristotle contended. However, Aristotle affirmed that, as knowledge-productive as it was, the most common function of metaphor was to spruce up literal ways of thinking and speaking. Remarkably, this latter position of Aristotle became the mindset with respect to metaphor in Western society at large, continuing on to this day. But since 1977, when a seminal study (Pollio, Barlow, Fine, and Pollio 1977) showed that speakers of English uttered, on average, 3,000 novel verbal metaphors and 7,000 idioms per week, it has become clear that metaphor is hardly an option to literal language. It constitutes the core of cognition and communication.

Defining metaphor semiotically poses an interesting dilemma. In the metaphorical *Rabbit* used for an automobile, there are two referents, not one, that are related to each other:

- There is the primary referent, the automobile itself, which is known as the *topic* of the metaphor.

- Then there is another referent, *rabbit*, which is known as the *vehicle* of the metaphor.

- Their correlation creates a new meaning, called the *ground*, which is not the simple sum of the meanings of the two referents. This is shown as a simple formula: *The automobile is a rabbit.*

However, it is not the denotative meanings of the vehicle that are transferred to the topic, but rather its connotations. So, the *rabbit* in the above formula does not stand for the denotative meaning of *rabbit*, but rather the characteristics perceived in rabbits. So, in effect, there is an exchange of domains in metaphor. Metaphor reveals a basic tendency of the human mind to think of certain referents (the topic of the metaphor) in terms of others (the vehicle). The question now becomes: Is there any psychological motivation for this? In the case of *The automobile is a rabbit*, the probable reason for correlating two semantically unrelated referents seems to be the *de facto* perception that humans and/or human-made objects and animals are interconnected in the natural scheme of things. Metaphor thus reveals a puzzling knack for establishing similarities among dissimilar things, interconnecting them within mind-space.

Among the first to point this out was Vico (2.2.3), the philosopher who saw metaphor as the unique ability of humanity to interconnect things and events in the world. Before Vico, metaphor was viewed as a manifestation of *analogy* (or, more precisely, as a form of *comparison*). In logic, analogy is an inductive form of reasoning that asserts that if two or more entities are similar in one or more respects, then a probability exists that they will be similar in other respects. For Vico, on the other hand, metaphor was hardly an analogy; it was the primary tool humans use for creating analogies themselves and, thus, for thinking about otherwise unknowable things. Once a connection between referents is made metaphorically, it produces a concept that seems to possess a "necessary logic" by virtue of the association itself.

3.3.2 Other rhetorical devices

In addition to metaphor, there are a host of verbal techniques that advertisers use effectively in generating textuality. Some of these are as follows (Dyer 1982: 151-182):

- *Jingles and Slogans*: These have the effect of reinforcing the recognizability of a brand name, since they tend quickly to make their way into communal memory: *Have a great day, at McDonald's, Join the Pepsi Generation,* etc.

- *Use of the Imperative Form:* This creates the effect of advice coming from an unseen authoritative source: *Pump some iron, Trust your senses*, etc.

- *Formulas*. Formulas create the effect of making meaningless statements sound truthful: *Triumph has a bra for the way you are; A Volkswagen is a Volkswagen;* etc.

- *Alliteration*. The alliteration, or repetition, of sounds increases the likelihood that a brand name will be remembered: *The Superfree sensation* (alliteration of *s*); *Guinness is good for you;* (alliteration of *g*), etc.;

- *Absence of language*. Some ads strategically avoid the use of any language whatsoever, suggesting, by implication, that the product speaks for itself. As Dyer (1982: 170) puts it, the absence of language in certain ad texts "has the effect of making us think that meaningful reality lies directly behind the signs once we have succeeded in deciphering them."

- *Intentional omission*. This technique is based on the fact that secrets grab our attention: *Don't tell your friends about ...; Do you know what she's wearing?* ; etc.

- *Parallelism*. This is the repetition of linguistic patterns (sentences, phrases, etc.): *It's longer/It's slimmer/It's surprisingly mild* (advertisement for *More* cigarettes).

In television and radio commercials the tone of voice, the sentence structure, and the use of various verbal ploys (jingles, slogans, etc.) are used to enhance product image. The tone of voice can be seductive, friendly, cheery, insistent, foreboding, etc. as required by product textuality. The sentence structure of ads and commercials is usually informal and colloquial, unless the ad is about some "high-class" product (e.g. a *BMW* automobile, a *Parker* pen, etc.), in which case it is normally more elegant and refined. In general, the type of sentence style used in ads and commercials is, as we have seen, a short imperative phrase - *Pump some iron, Trust your senses* - or aphoristic statement - *Somewhere inside, romance blossoms*. Advertising also borrows discourse styles to suit its purposes: a commercial can take the form of an interview; a testimonial on the part of a celebrity; an official format (*Name:* Mary; *Age:* 15; *Problem:* acne), and so on.

The intentional use of traditional *poetic* devices is widespread in all forms of advertising. These are employed in particular in the creation of captions and headlines (Tash 1979). For instance, an ad designed to attract business in the *New York Times* in 1977 beings as follows:

Franchisers

Find

Franchisees

Fast

Clearly, the alliteration of four consecutive /f/ sounds creates a kind of tongue-twisting effect that is pleasurable in itself. Also, the consecutive sequence of a trisyllabic word followed by a monosyllabic one creates a catchy rhythm and thus adds flowing tinge to the headline. Often the alliteration is morphological, i.e. it occurs at the word level through the repetition of the same word but with a different meaning. For example, in the 1970s, *Sudden Beauty* products used the following headline in a variety of magazines:

> *How to make up*
> *Without make-up!*

Such poetic license is not only appealing; it is memorable and it conveys its message in a form that produces its own type of aesthesia. Personification is also a common device that has its own kind of logic. In an ad prepared by the Insurance Bureau of Canada, the headline *Let's Free Enterprise* is accompanied by the picture of a bird flying out of a cage. The personification of *Enterprise* is, of course, a poetic device that was clearly used to reinforce the message.

Sometimes an idiom or a proverb is altered them in order to generate certain meanings (Tash 1979: 229). An example of this was *TWA's* extremely successful ad campaign of the 1970s which used the following headline:

> *TWA's*
> *Spring Sale*
> *on the Rockies*

The quasi-idiom *on the Rockies* is, of course, a slight modification of *on the rocks*, which can mean either "in trouble" (as in *My life is on the rocks*) or "with ice" (as in *I'll have my Martini on the rocks*). It is the second meaning that is selected by *TWA* as could be seen in the pictorial part the ads - generally showing skiers with their skis and poles leaning against a tree as if they were hanging out in a bar waiting for their drinks.

In a sales pitch for its newspaper, the *New York Times* created the following headline during the early 1980s:

> *Clarity begins at home*
> *with the home delivery of*
> *the New York Times*

The line *Clarity begins at home* is an obvious modification of the proverb *Charity begins at home.* This clever use of phraseology imparts a sense of proverbial qualities to the product at the same time that it generates a high connotative index.

3.4 Nonverbal techniques

The discussion of the surface presentation of the *Marilyn Peach, Versus, Iron, Volupté,* and *L'Effleur* ads focused primarily on visual signifiers, because these were the critical ones in leading to the underlying subtexts. As our interpretations show, facial expression in particular is extremely important as a visual signifier. The expression on the female in the *Marilyn Peach* ad, or of the males in the *Versus* ad, helped us unlock the underlying meanings of the texts. In the *Iron Cologne* ad the male's expression conveys domination and control; the female's submissive sensuality. The face is, clearly, a primary source of emotional communication. The lack of eye contact in the above ads also conveys a definite message. Looking in the eyes is a sign of love and affection. Looking away and closing one's eyes is a sign of sexual rapture and reverie.

Visual images in advertising are absolutely critical in reinforcing product textuality. People can picture faces and images much more accurately and quickly than they can recall words. This is also why cartoon characters, computer graphics, and the like are used to endorse or represent products. Mouthwash bottles dance across the screen; automobiles turn into animals; etc.

3.4.1 Modeling

Another salient aspect of the *Marilyn Peach, Versus,* and *Iron Cologne* ads is the *bodily* forms of the personages - the females have a soft, slim body form, and the males a muscular and slim one. The strategy of representing prototypes such as these can be called *modeling*. In the above ads, the bodies of the characters are all modeled in a specific way - as slim, muscular (in the case of the men), sleek, etc. This is due to an association of *slimness* with *attractiveness*. In our culture we tend to perceive corpulence negatively. But in all cultures, body size is not just a matter of physique, but also an issue of aesthetics. In contemporary Western society, the slim, lean look is a prerequisite for attractiveness for both males and females. The margin of flexibility from any idealized thinness model is larger for males than it is for females; but males must additionally strive to develop a muscular look.

Modeling can take a variety of forms. Television and radio commercials based on jingles, for instance, are designed to model some rhythmic quality of the product or some aesthetic characteristic of its signification system with some catchy, memorable tune. This is why *Coca Cola* and *Pepsi*, for instance, have consistently created commercials based on songs that could be easily remembered and hummed. They functioned as musical models representing their products in an aesthetically pleasing way.

Consider, as another case-in-point, a *Coco* perfume ad found in many magazines in the mid-1990s. *Coco* is an expensive women's perfume. The initial analytical step on the path leading to the subtext created by this perfume's textuality consists in describing the iconic features of its surface text:

- The first thing that can be noted in the ad is a voluptuous, young woman dressed up to resemble a bird.

- She has a "tail;" she is tied down by a rope around her ankle; she is seated at the top of a staircase.

- The background is pitch dark, making both her and the oversized bottle of the perfume she is holding up stand out distinctly.

- She is clad scantily in sexy fishnet pantyhose and long black gloves.

- She is looking straight into the viewer's eye.

This *modeling* of the female figure is a key to decoding the ad. Incidentally, the word *Coco* itself reinforces the bird signifier since it is clearly imitative of the sounds a bird might be perceived to make. The connotations of the visual layout, the modeling of the female, and the implied meanings of the brand name open up one possible route to the subtext. These features evoke such connotations as "crazy," "wild," "unconventional," uninhibited." They can also be interpreted in terms of two other signifieds, namely "infatuated" and "obsessed." Furthermore, *Coco* is an abbreviation for *cocaine*, which is not only a narcotic, but also an aphrodisiacal intoxicant.

These considerations raise the following questions:

- Who is the woman?
- Why is she dressed up as a bird?
- Why does she have a rope around her ankle?
- Who or what is holding the rope?
- Why is it so dark?
- Why is she dressed in this way?

Perfume is designed to be a sexual stimulant, a means for enhancing sexual attractiveness through the olfactory channel. At a surface level, the ad must be related to the product's function. And, indeed, the woman in the ad appears to be sexually desirable. Like a female bird sending out olfactory mating signals, we can almost smell her sexual scent synesthetically.

Her bodily schema is indicative of voyeuristic poise. She is seemingly ready and approachable by the male of the species. The *dark* tone of the ad is symbolic of the night, when sex and seduction purportedly take place. Darkness also connotes evil, mystery, danger, fear, and excitement. The modeling of the human female as a bird is a deeply embedded image in our culture. In English slang, for example, a young, pretty girl is called a *chick*; and the expressions *stuffing a bird* and *getting tail* mean "to have sex with a woman." The woman in the ad has black feathers, suggesting a syntagmatic chain of nefarious connotations. Black birds are associated with voraciousness, carnivorousness, insatiability. The woman, by implication, is perceived to be ravenous for sexual mating, with the same kinds of sexual instincts of a bird of prey.

But the ad is suggestive of many more subtexts. Its connotative index is at a maximum, given its high degree of ambiguity and ambivalence. In fact, the whole scenario can elicit various connotative chains. One is the *woman-as-pet* metaphor, i.e. the view of woman as a "pet" adored, pampered, and "maintained" (enslaved) for sexual amusement and satisfaction. This is why she is tied down, making her escape impossible. The staircase on which she is "perched," moreover, is symbolic of both a pedestal of veneration and a phallic structure. Her bodily posture is imitative of a woman who is sexually "on top." Another possible interpretative line of reasoning is that of *woman-as-sacrificial-victim*. On top of a black altar, she is worshipped and offered as a sacrifice to a male god. It is also relevant to note that the rope tied around her ankle is spermatozoid in shape and that it is colored red, a symbol of sexuality and eroticism. Is she tied in sexual bondage to some person, or to some irresistible force form below? The ambiguity of the rope's point of origin is powerful - the source of her enslavement may be the dark forces of nature, some dominating male, or even the woman herself. We will never know because the rope fades away into the dark background.

Let us now consider a few other visual cues that lead to other kinds of interpretations:

- The woman is barefoot, which is suggestive of fertility and of the woman's biological role as mother. The woman is, in fact, holding the bottle of *Coco* next to her face and breast, as she would a child.

- There is further ambiguity in the fact that the woman's bare back, shoulders, and scanty attire are highly erotic; but her slightly turned position is suggestive of modesty. The paradigmatic juxtaposition of eroticism and modesty give the woman great sexual allure.

- The oversized bottle of *Coco*, with its vivid amber color, juxtaposed against the dark background, is highly suggestive of fire and flames, and, thus, of burning desire.

As a final comment, it would seem that the woman is surrounded by a surreal void. The female "bird" appears mysteriously out of nothingness, as in a dream. Is she a figment of the libidinous imagination? Is the subtext, therefore, simply that of an erotic dream which wearing the perfume, or buying it for your loved one, will make possible? Surrealism, as Bachand (1992: 5) remarks, "has been and still is a great inspiration to advertisers."

The *Coco* ad, and *Chanel* advertisements and commercials generally, are always ambiguous and surreal. They have perhaps the highest connotative indexes of all lifestyle ads. Like symbolism and surrealism in visual art, they tap into underlying archetypal themes, instincts, and feelings that are beyond the threshold of consciousness. A while back, *Chanel* had a commercial for the perfume *Egoiste*, showing a group of females (or was it the same female dressed in different clothes?) opening and shutting doors in a building and shouting *égoiste* over and over. Without going into the details of the commercial here, suffice it to say that its emotive force resided in its surreal and ambiguous quality: Were the women blaming men for their macho sexual egoism? Were they "opening" and "closing" their sexual organs?

The elicitation of feeling through symbolic forms is a powerful means for making and for extracting meaning. Thus, in a basic sense, the *Chanel* ads and commercials are works of "art." The difference between such works and, say, the works of a Rodin, a Renoir, or a Picasso is, in our view, that they are not "searching" for some meaning to life. They are simply tapping into the unconscious domain of the mind in an attempt to associate its connotative dynamism, trivially, with a product.

Another example of the use of surrealism, as Judith Williamson (1996) has astutely pointed out, was an ad campaign by *Benson & Hedges* cigarettes of a number of years ago. Surrealism was a twentieth century art movement that emphasized the role of the unconscious in creative activity. The movement spread all over the world and flourished in the United States during World War II (1939-

1945). Surrealists often employed abstract and fantastic shapes and forms, with a great variety of content and technique. Their main objective was to give form to the world of dreams. *Benson & Hedges* ads like the *Mousetrap,* the *Birdcage*, and the *Christmas Tree* were designed in the surrealist style, with the product taking its form from its surroundings. This created a "surrealist puzzle," thus greatly raising the connotative index of the product. Williamson (1996: 398) puts it eloquently as follows:

> It is the very difficulty in understanding the images, and the absence of obvious connections, which indicates the genuinely cultured status of the ads, and therefore, of the product. The ads are visual puzzles, they imply meanings one doesn't have access to. This suggests 'High Art' and thereby, exclusivity. A product for the discerning, the tasteful, the few.

In general, ads and commercials for perfume, clothes, drinks, and other lifestyle and "image-enhancing" products play on our feelings of ambiguity and aesthetic sensibilities. This is why the right faces and body styles of models in ads and commercials are always crucial in getting the ad to work. This is why, for instance, the female in the *Coco* ad is staring tantalizingly at her prey, the viewer. Her face is a powerful carrier of the state of sexual arousal. As Paul Ekman (e.g. 1985 and 1988) has shown, the facial text can be broken down into its components: eyebrow position, eye shape, mouth shape, nostril size, etc. which in various combinations determine the expression of the face. It is, indeed, possible to write a "grammar" of the face which shows less cross-cultural variation than do language grammars. The features of the female's face are clearly representative of a sexual state of readiness and willingness. The eye contact that the female is making with the viewer is particularly forceful as a sexual signifier. Her pupils are dilated. It is a documented fact by psychologists that the female face is perceived as more sexually attractive when the pupils are dilated. In fact, in earlier times in Italy, extracts of the drug *belladonna* were used for its cosmetic effect, given that it produces extreme dilation of the pupils. This drug is now used by eye doctors to facilitate eye examinations; but its cosmetic applications explain the origin of its name, which in Italian means "beautiful woman" (Sebeok 1994).

3.4.2 A synthesis

Perfumes and colognes are surrogates for natural scents and are typically presented as improvements on Nature. As Vestergaard and Schrøder (1985: 159) remark, such ads proclaim their product as "somehow superior to their natural source," offering, in effect, "to lend nature a hand."

As is the case with all lifestyle products, perfume or cologne assumes a personality in advertising. Some are portrayed as "rugged" and "virile," like *Brut*; others as "smooth" and "refined," like *Chanel*. *Drakkar noir* obviously appeals to the dark, macabre, sinister side of masculine sexual fantasies. It is evocative of mythic portrayals - Don Juan, Dracula, and even Mephistopheles, the darkest of all. The guttural sound of *Drakkar* - obviously coined in imitation of Dracula, the deadly vampire who would mesmerize his sexual prey with a mere glance - is probably designed to evoke, unconsciously, both a surreptitious fear and a feeling of lust in the viewer. Is the *Drakkar noir* brand name alluding to the intertext of *Faust* selling his soul to the devil so that he could satisfy all his desires? Does wearing *Drakkar noir* constitute a Faustian pact with the devil to achieve erotic power? There is certainly much more to cologne than smell in this ad-mediated world!

In sum, as we have seen , advertising textuality consists of two orders of signification:

(1) a surface textual, conscious, denotative one;

(2) a subtextual, unconscious, connotative one.

The mythic themes and metaphors that are implied in the subtext fit into a coherent system of signification created by the textuality and personality of the product itself. As Alsted and Larsen (1991: 7-8) aptly observe, lifestyle ads in particular are "complex signifying texts" because they are grounded in a cultural substratum fertile with mythic and metaphorical connotation.

Consider, as one final illustrative case-in-point, yet one other *Chanel* ad that was found in magazines in the late 1990s. This one showed:

- a woman standing on a park bench holding a water hose;

- but she is dressed as if she were about to go out "on the town;"

- except for her casual shoes.

It is not necessary to go here into a complete decoding of this ad. Only one suggestive line of interpretation will be discussed here.

The background in the ad is that of a garden. Does this have any connotative meaning? The answer is, of course, that in our culture, gardens frequently have mythic connotations. Could this garden be suggestive of the "Garden of Eden?" Let us, in fact, assume the hypothesis that the subtextual level alludes to the temptation theme in the Book of Genesis. Are there any other indications that this is a plausible hunch? The iconic cue that gives it away is the hose in the form of a snake that the woman is holding.

As in the *Marilyn Peach* ad, the devil came to Eve in the body of a snake to prod her on to tempt Adam. Adam, of course, is the possessor of a phallus that "ejaculates" in the same way that the hose does in the hand of Eve. The "Garden of Eden" intertext in this ad and all its sexual-erotic connotations make it a psychologically powerful one. The expression of satisfaction, domination, and control on the face of the woman reinforces this subtext.

Chapter IV
Advertising and culture

We live in a world ruled by fictions of every kind - mass merchandising, advertising, politics conducted as a branch of advertising, the instant translation of science and technology into popular imagery, the increasing blurring and intermingling of identities within the realm of consumer goods, the preempting of any free or original imaginative response to experience by the television screen. We live inside an enormous novel. For the writer in particular it is less and less necessary for him to invent the fictional content of his novel. The fiction is already there. The writer's task is to invent the reality.

J. G. Ballard (1930-)

4. Introductory remarks

The feature that characterizes the business of modern advertising is that it has joined forces with marketing science in the business of getting products and services from producers to consumers in the most effective way possible. The main activity of marketing science today involves ascertaining ways in which product image for a specific group of buyers can best be enhanced. A basic marketing research technique is the survey of test markets to determine the potential acceptance of products or services before they are advertised. Through a process of careful questioning and investigation it is possible for an advertiser to learn what a consumer likes about an ad, a commercial, or an ad campaign. This process is, needless to say, fundamentally a semiotic one. The work of the advertiser and marketer is, fundamentally, the work of the semiotician. Since consumers can choose from a huge variety of products and services, the process of ascertaining what signification system will make products and services attractive to customers has become a crucial one in today's marketplace. Marketers are involved, in effect, more in *selling signs* than in selling products.

The goal of this chapter is to extend semiotic analysis into the domain of cultural analysis. Specifically, the goal here is to show

how semiotic theory and philosophy can inform the current debate on advertising.

4.1 Market testing the product's signification system

We will start with a glance at the research side of advertising. *Market research* is the scientific enterprise that aims to determine the probable users of a product or service. The results from the research lead to concrete suggestions for product development, including which products are to be manufactured. This allows manufacturers to meet the demands of the public by adding new products, changing existing ones, and dropping others. It also allows manufacturers to determine the best system of distribution of products and services and what the optimal pricing for these is.

Most business firms hire advertising agencies to create their advertisements and place them in the various media. In most cases, individual advertisements form part of an advertising campaign, which as we have seen, constitutes a systematic method of advertising products and services that may run for several months, or more, and that usually involves more than one medium. The objective of the campaign may be to demonstrate a product's superiority over competing brands, to change the image of the product or company, or to achieve some other goal. The agency must also determine the target market - i.e. the people who are likely users of a product and at whom the advertising will be aimed. Finally, the agency has to estimate how much money and time will be needed to carry out the campaign. Information gathered from consumers provides the basis for determining the kinds of people at whom to aim advertisements, the types of signification systems to use, and in which media to place the ads. The chief kinds of market research include: (1) market research, (2) motivation research, and (3) media research.

Market research aims to determine the target group on the basis of the age, sex, income, and occupation of potential consumers and their reactions to various brands. This type of information helps advertisers decide as to the best way to present the features of their products. Motivation research attempts to find out why people buy certain products, through personal interviews, during which certain techniques developed by psychologists and sociologists are used. By discovering the motives for people's buying behavior, advertisers hope to find the most effective style of presentation to use in their advertisements. Media research involves measuring the size and makeup of radio and TV audiences at different times of the day, and of circulations of publications. Advertisers use information on audience size and makeup in selecting media in which to place ads. They then prepare a media plan that will give an effective combination of *reach* - the number of people who will see or hear the advertisement - and *frequency* - the number of times that they will see or hear it.

In effect, the advertising agencies cannot show that an ad or commercial makes an individual buy a product or service, or that the individual's behavior has been affected. Rather, as Berger (2000: 3) aptly puts it, "we can say that advertising has a collective impact; that is, it affects people in general."

4.1.1 Case study 1: Determining signification systems

The goal of marketing research is, essentially, unraveling what systems of signification fit best for a product or service and which media can optimally be employed to deliver the systems. In effect, marketing research is *applied semiotic research*. Two case studies in which the authors of this manual have been involved can be used to illustrate this very fact. The first case study involved a well-known baby food company, which had decided to introduce a new brand, X. The project aimed to ascertain the connotative potential that X had for typical mothers.

To determine the signification system of X paradigmatically, a group of subjects was asked to compare X to two other well-known brand name baby food products - which we will call Y and Z - using the three words that best summed up their attitudes currently vis-à-vis commercially produced baby foods, and three words that would have best summed up their attitudes five years ago. These were subsequently discussed with the group. The subjects were then asked the following:

- What do you see as the strengths and weaknesses of the brands?

- What, if anything, does the brand offer that makes it unique?

- What one aspect of baby food or baby nutrition do you feel the brand excels in?

- What does each brand specialize in/focus on?

- What are your reactions on being exposed to the range of products within each brand, establishing whether or not the range is extensive enough and what additional products, if any, you would like to see?

In the case of the brand under study, X, the subjects were asked specifically: (1) what their reactions to it were; (2) what it stood for in their minds; and (3) what it brought to the overall line in terms of quality associations. Then, five "connotation-establishing" techniques were used:

(1) a *collage* technique, by which the subjects were asked to cut out pictures from magazines that best represented the product, gluing them onto a surface;

(2) an *imaginary world* technique, by which each subject was required to compare each brand to a world or land in terms of its topography, climate, architecture, society, values, lifestyle, attitudes towards child-rearing;

(3) a *portrait chinois* technique, by which each subject was asked to identify each brand as a musical instrument, an animal, a film genre, a book, a weather system, a landscape, a gesture, an emotion, etc.;

(4) a *picture association* technique, whereby each subject was required to picture a typical mother and baby who might use each brand, drawing and describing the home and the baby's room, and indicating how she pictured the manufacturers in this scenario;

(5) a *slogan* technique, whereby each subject was asked to invent a slogan for each brand that best summed it up regardless of any slogans used in advertising for this purpose.

The subjects were also asked to indicate what advertising, if any, they recalled having seen, read, or heard for any of the brands, and to comment on packaging, marketing initiatives, and expectations for each brand.

The reason for the above questions was, of course, to flesh out as many relevant connotations as possible associated with the products. After this, the group was asked to comment on a number of advertising concepts developed by the manufacturers, including:

- immediate reactions (first thoughts and feelings);

- understanding of the message (what impressions each one got from the brand);

- relevance of the message (Does it meet your needs or not?);

- uniqueness of the brand in relation to existing brands and adult food;

- attractive and unattractive aspects of the product;

- overall feeling (Does it strike you as personally meaningful and motivating or not?)

After revealing that these were all potential ways of communicating about X, they were asked which brand was:

- the most involving and motivating and why;

- the one that they would most want for their babies over all other alternatives;

- the one that fits best with what X could stand for in the future;

- how they would rank the brands X, Y, and Z.

The subjects were made up of 8 focus groups, 4 in each of New York City and Cleveland with participants recruited according to the brands they used and income level - lower income defined as annual household incomes of $30,000 or less; higher income as annual household incomes of $50,000 or more. The participants were all mothers of babies aged 3 to 24 months, who purchased baby food on a regular basis, serving jarred baby food at least five times a week. There was mix of working and non-working mothers and of mothers with one child versus more than one child in each group.

We will not go into the minute details that were collected here, nor will we break down the results quantitatively. Our purpose is simply to illustrate the kind of methodology that can be used to establish signification systems for products. Overall, it was found that the most relevant connotations to the mothers were the following two:

- Baby food should allow mothers to express a sense of love, warmth, comfort, and security through the feeding event.

- Like adult foods, it should offer the opportunity to introduce babies to the cuisine of one's culture.

With regard to packaging, there was a sense expressed even on the part of X users that the X packaging was old-fashioned, boring, outdated, and stodgy. Part of the problem, they suggested, was the lack of excitement in product descriptions used. Overall, it was felt that X should update its image through its packaging.

With regard to the concepts, all mothers felt that baby food manufacturers should ensure that their products: (1) help babies develop healthy eating habits by providing natural-tasting food, and (2) contain essential nutrients.

The perception of X as a brand associated with warmth, bonding, and the family is the signification system that best suits it. It was also felt that X continue emphasizing this system, not trying to expand its image to include the connotative chains generated by Y and Z. Overall, it would seem that for most mothers, X's traditional signification system has a high connotative index. The only area of change would seem to be in packaging, which was seen unanimously as in need of updating.

4.1.2 Case study 2: Co-branding

The second case study was commissioned by a company that operates a number of co-branded restaurant chains. The restaurant chains are labeled X, Y, and Z. A need was identified within the company to establish what is communicated to consumers by using combinations of brand names (X + Y, X + Z, Y + Z), in order to develop a long-term strategy for the company's portfolio. The overall objective of the study, therefore, was to establish the signification system generated at co-branded sites. The specific questions guiding the research issues were:

- Does co-branding dilute the signification system of individual brands or cause confusion?

- Are there real branding benefits or only operational benefits?

- What are the ingredients for successful co-branding?

- Can the individual signification system of each brand be maintained within the context of co-branding?

- Are there service performance requirements for each brand, and can staff distinguish between these and deliver different service patterns?

An evaluation of each combination of brands was conducted by an integration of semiotic analysis with anthropological ethnographic research. A semiotic analysis was undertaken beforehand of printed materials (menus, print ads, on-premises materials, internal documents and consumer communications), the physical appearance of outlets (design, layout, seating, spacing, decor). The analysis was complemented by ethnographic research involving systematic observation at three co-branded sites:

- X at X Plus (= proposed new branding) using the new decor and logos

- Y at X Plus, using the older 1997 decor and logos

- Y with Z

Advance notice was given to the manager at each site and the researcher introduced himself upon arriving. The researcher sat down at a table affording a full view of the premises and the service counter. While observation sessions lasted approximately six hours, lunchtime (11:30 to 14:30) was the period of reference for all three locations. A 15 to 20 minute discussion was also carried out with the manager at each site at some point during the observation period. Stops were also made at four other Y sites located en route to the three main sites to gather comparative data.

Co-branding need not dilute the signification systems of individual brands or cause confusion, provided it is additive. For co-branding to be additive, the systems of each brand should ideally be integrated into the new designation with both retaining their whole connotative range. If this cannot be maintained, the "default" brand meaning should be the one that "takes over" the other. This means, for instance, that in an X restaurant serving Y products, the X meanings should be kept intact with the Y meanings added on, and vice versa.

There can be real branding benefits as well as operational ones with additive co-branding. The co-branding of *Chapters* with *Starbucks* illustrates this, with both sharing connotations of order and organization, with the intellectual connotations of *Chapters* being additive to the gourmet ones of *Starbucks*. This additive effect means that co-branding *Chapters* with *Starbucks* results in a "mind-body" signification system, focusing on the individual who enjoys the finer things in life, and is cultured in a well-rounded way.

The prerequisites for successful co-branding are therefore two brands with some connotations that are shared and others that are different but compatible and complementary. The individual meanings of each brand can be maintained within the context of co-branding. However, this implies that the signification systems of each must be constantly reinforced and that no changes be implemented that may undermine the value of the "default" brand.

It was found that the different service requirements of X and Y are compatible. Service at X requires attentiveness within the context of the ordering and dining experiences while service at Y requires attentiveness within the context of the ordering and preparation experiences. Thus, X and Y appeared to be not only compatible but consistent with achieving additive co-branding through X Plus and Y Plus. The common sign linking the two was attentiveness, which can be delivered within both the X Plus and Y Plus contexts. It was found, however, that there were signification system differences with regard to Z, especially between Y and Z, resulting in a subtractive effect for Y.

While there is no evidence that the availability of Y products in X Plus outlets is subtractive, whether or not there would be additive value in promoting Y products more overtly is unclear. However, the effect may be additive, since Y shares values of cleanliness, safety and quality with X and may add a dimension of youthfulness and individualism to the new amalgamated signification system. The Y Plus co-branding experience turned out to be more clearly an example of additive co-branding. As executed, the core system of Y would be maintained with the availability of X products underscoring existing quality connotations and being an extension of the principle of freedom of choice. As in the case of X Plus, however, care must be taken to preserve all of the elements of the Y experience intact in the future.

The Y serving Z experience turned out, as mentioned, to be subtractive. Behavior observed in this co-branded environment suggests that there is inconsistency between the meanings of Y and Z. Y customers seemed to resolve this inconsistency by ignoring Z. However, the more successfully Z is promoted within the Y environment, the greater the risk that the signification system of Y will be changed from that of a superior fast-food outlet offering freedom of choice to that of an inferior fast-food outlet offering poor nutrition and standardization.

The follow-up research areas were then recommended:

- to conduct qualitative research using projective techniques to understand the current equity of Z and provide guidance in terms of how best to develop the brand, either within a stand-alone or co-branded context;

- to conduct quantitative exit interviews at key co-branded sites to measure customer reactions and brand perceptions to validate the hypotheses of this evaluation;

- to extend the semiotic and ethnographic evaluation to other co-branding contexts, both existing and potential.

Co-branding is, in a manner of speaking, a kind of "semiotic chemical mixture," whereby the connotative meanings of two signs fuse into a new one. For any co-branding mixture to be additive, it is imperative to ensure that the signification systems of each brand individually are maintained.

A semiotic analysis of the printed materials provided by the company suggested the following. First, X, which is intended to be a chain of casual family restaurants, generates the following connotative chain:

- a homey environment
- a relaxed, non-urban environment
- freedom from stress
- freedom from pretensions
- a change from home
- a change that is clean, safe and efficient
- different without being exotic
- tradition.

Its menu complements this chain, since it generates the following connotative signifieds:

- healthy, nutritious meals with rotisserie chicken emphasizing protein prepared in a relatively healthy manner;

- meals the whole family can enjoy, with chicken being almost universally acceptable and a safe choice.

Y, which is intended to be a chain of quick service restaurants, generates the following connotative signifieds instead:

- a chain where someone is responsible, conveyed through the use of a personal name (as in the case of *Wendy's* and *McDonald's*);

- homey, implied by the use of the genitive in its brand name;

- speed and efficiency through the use of a single word (rather than *Burger King* or X);

- but personalization too, through the use of a first name (as in the case of *Wendy's*, but not *McDonald's*);

- an informal and youthful appeal, based on a personal relationship on a first-name basis, rather than the all-family appeal of X.

Its menu complements this system, since it generates the following connotations:

- somewhere young people and people young at heart can enjoy the foods they like, the logo placing the emphasis on the food rather than the environment;

- an aspirational appeal to teens and young adults who want to distance themselves from the child orientation of *McDonald's*;

- a way for adults who are concerned about what they eat to feel good about foods they enjoy;

- good quality fast food, the method of preparation distinguishing Y from junk food;

- individuality and a recognition of the existence of personal preferences.

Z, which is intended to be a chain of fast food restaurants serving chicken, generates the following connotative signifieds instead:

- the speed and efficiency of a fast food outlet with its use of a single name;

- lacks the sense of someone being responsible (Z being an unusual surname with institutional overtones);

- lacks the personal touch of a first name;

- theoretically conveys trust, stability and positive values, although the association with fried chicken contradicts this.

Its menu complements this system, since it signifies:

- fast food, with the logo focusing on chicken as the source, without much redeeming value;

- unhealthy food / junk food;

- an indulgence for individuals who are not discriminating about quality and nutrition;

- lower socio-economic status and obesity because of the brash visual approach and overt connection with fried chicken.

In sum, from a semiotic perspective, it turned out that only concern for the company would co-branding Y and Z, which could be subtractive. For the co-branding to work, Y must remain the "default" brand - i.e. all the connotative meanings of Y must remain intact, with the Z meanings being added on. This also entails that all else remains intact - e.g. that Y service be provided.

4.1.3 Other techniques

The discussion in the previous chapter about connotative indexes suggests a method that, as far as we know, has probably never been used in market research. The method would be to simply ask subjects ask what a particular ad means. The ability of respondents to figure out the subtextual features of ads would be inversely proportional to the ad's effectiveness: i.e. the more the respondents are aware of the ad's subtext, the less effective will it be as a persuasive text. The power of the text lies in its ambiguity and dense connotative layering. An ad whose signifieds can be easily figured out works mainly on a denotative level, and its overall effect is thus minimal.

The effectiveness of high connotative indexes is seen easily at Christmas time when gifts for children become highly charged with connotations. At no time in recent history have the effects of connotation been so conspicuous as during the 1983 Christmas shopping season. If the reader has forgotten, that was the period of the "Cabbage Patch" doll craze. Hordes of parents were prepared to pay almost anything to get one of those dolls for their daughters. Scalpers offered the suddenly and unexplainably "out-of-stock" dolls (a marketing ploy?) for hundreds of dollars through the classified ads. Grown adults fought each other in line-ups to get one of the few remaining dolls left in stock at some mall toy outlet.

How could a toy, a simple doll, have caused such mass hysteria? To a semiotician, only something with a high connotative index could have possibly triggered such intense commotion. The Cabbage Patch dolls came with "adoption papers." This was a concrete clue as to what the dolls really signified. Each doll was given a name - taken at random from 1938 state of Georgia birth records - which, like any act of naming, conferred upon it a human personality. And, thanks to computerized production, no two dolls were manufactured alike, as different from each other as two human beings. The doll became alive in the child's mind, providing the precious human contact that children living in nuclear families with both parents working desperately need. Dolls are "people substitutes." In some cultures, one is purported to be able to cause some physical or psychological effect on a person by doing something to a doll constructed to resemble that person. In our culture, children, and adults for that matter, "talk" to their dolls, who are felt to lend a receptive ear to their owners' needs and frustrations. Dolls answer a deep need for human contact. No wonder, then, that the Cabbage Patch episode was such an hysterical one. Parents did not buy a simple doll, they bought their child a sibling.

Perhaps the most effective technique that can be used by marketers to flesh out what an ad text means or connotes to people is the so-called *semantic differential,* invented in 1957 by C. E. Osgood, G. J. Suci, and P. H. Tannenbaum - a technique used widely by semioticians interested in advertising. The technique consists in posing a series of questions about a specific concept - *Is it good or bad? weak or strong?* etc. - as seven-point scales, with the opposing adjectives at each end. The answers are then analyzed statistically in order to sift out any general pattern from them. Consider a hypothetical example. Suppose that various subjects are asked to evaluate the concept *President* in terms of scales such as the following:

	1	2	3	4	5	6	7	
young								old
practical								idealistic
modern								traditional
attractive								bland
friendly								stern

An informant who feels that the *President* should be modern, would place a mark towards the *modern* end of the *modern-traditional* scale. One who feels that a *President* should not be too young or old, would place a mark near the middle of the *young-old* scale. An informant who feels that a *President* should be bland, would place a mark towards the *bland* end of the *attractive-bland* scale; and so on. If a large number of informants were asked to rate the term *President* in this way, then it would be possible to draw an ideal profile of the *presidency* in terms of the statistically-significant variations in connotation that the term evokes. Interestingly, research utilizing the semantic differential has shown that, while the meanings of most concepts are subject to personal interpretation and subjective feelings, the range of variation in interpretation is not random, but forms a socially-based pattern. In other words, the use of this technique has shown that connotation is constrained by culture: e.g. the word *noise* turns out to be a highly emotional concept for the Japanese, who rate it consistently at the ends of the scales presented to them; whereas it is a fairly neutral concept for Americans who place it in the mid range of the scales. This same technique can, clearly, be used to flesh out the meanings of any ad text presented to subjects: e.g. by using scales such as *sexy-unsexy, friendly-unfriendly, aggressive-unaggressive,* etc. one can flesh out the connotations that a text will elicit.

4.2 Advertising culture

As mentioned previously (1.3.3), the media used in advertising influence cognitive style and thus are critical shapers of cultural worldview. One manifest effect of advertising, for example, has been the *juvenilization* of Western culture at large - i.e. the emphasis on being, staying, thinking, and looking young at any age. That is a primary signification system built into many products.

The roots of this phenomenon can be traced to the first decades of the twentieth century, when for the first time in history a single economic system - the one that took shape after the Industrial Revolution of the nineteenth century - was capable of guaranteeing a certain level of affluence to increasingly larger segments of society.

With more wealth and leisure time at their disposal, common people became more inclined to live the good life. And with the economic capacity to improve their chances of staying healthier, and thus of living much longer than previous generations, a desire to preserve youth for a much longer period of life started to define the collective state of mind. This desire was nurtured by the messages that bombarded society from radio and print advertising in the early part of the century - messages that became more persuasive and widespread with the advent of television as a social text in the early 1950s. By the 1960s, the desire to be "young" not only meant the desire to stay and look healthier for a longer period of life, but also to act and think differently than "older" people. Being old meant being a part of the corrupt and morally fossilized "establishment," as the consumerist way of life was called by the counterculture dissidents of the era. By the end of the decade, the process of juvenilization had reached a critical mass, on the verge of becoming the defining feature of the mindset of an entire society.

As we saw (3.4.1), advertisers tapped into this process astutely and skillfully through the strategy of cooption. Being young and rebellious came to mean having a "cool look"; being anti-establishment and subversive came to mean wearing "hip clothes." "New" and "different" became the two key words of the advertising and marketing lexicon, coaxing people into buying goods, not because they necessarily needed them, but simply because they were "new," "cool," "hip." The underlying subtext of this clever discourse allowed buyers to believe that what they bought transformed them into ersatz revolutionaries without having to pay the social price of true nonconformity and dissent.

As the social critic Ewen (1988: 20) has aptly put it, the business world discovered fortuitously in that era how to incorporate the powerful images of youth protest into "the most constantly available lexicon from which many of us draw the visual grammar of our lives." It was those images that allowed advertisers and marketers to write a new lifestyle grammar with which they could easily build new semantic bridges between the product and the consumer's consciousness. This grammar has now systematized neomaniacal behaviors into the social structure of everyday life. This is why the constant craving for new items of consumption is no longer perceived as an aberration, but as part of the search for happiness, success, status, or beauty.

A society bombarded incessantly by advertising images is bound to become more and more susceptible to the effects of extreme forms of objectification. Because our consciousness is shaped by the type of stimuli and information to which we are exposed, the barrage of images generated by advertisements surreptitiously influence lifestyle and behavior, especially the perception of how many desirable material objects we should own and of how many pleasures we should be feeling.

Starting out as a simple "pitch" to make products and services better known in antiquity and the medieval periods, advertising has become a means of text-making that shapes values, aspirations, lifestyle. In a world where the marketplace dictates morality and ethics, it is little wonder that advertising and marketing run the social show, so to speak. It is ironic to contemplate that all this came about through the inadvertent efforts of those espousing Puritanical morality and ethics - the very antithesis of advertising Epicureanism. The Industrial Revolution of the nineteenth century was fostered and controlled initially by people with Puritanical values, who associated the accumulation of goods with the gaining of spiritual favor. As a consequence, such values unwittingly legitimized the emerging discourse of advertising at the time. The advertiser at first complemented the messages proclaimed by preachers. But shortly thereafter, with the spread of industrialism and the need to generate profits through increased consumption, the advertiser came progressively to take over the role of the preacher. And, indeed, there is a sermon in each advertisement. In a sense, advertisers devote themselves to proclaiming the consumerist faith and the means of attaining paradise on earth through consumption.

As we have attempted to show in this manual, to the semiotician advertising is extremely interesting, not because of its social implications, but because it manifests how signs are used in a specific domain of human meaning-making. The corollary to this interest has, of course, a practical implication - namely, that semiotics can be of great service to the study of advertising and marketing. The primary goal of this textbook has, in fact, been to show how semiotic method can be used in this domain both as a theoretical and a practical tool.

4.2.1 The advertising industry

Advertising has become a vital cog in the global consumerist-driven economic machine. The United States has the largest advertising industry in the world, with its center in New York City, where many of the major agencies have their headquarters. There are about 6,000 advertising agencies in the United States, ranging in size from one-person organizations to huge agencies with several thousand employees. An advertising agency's chief function, as we have discussed several times, is to create and place advertising for clients. Most large companies have an advertising department. In some, the department prepares all the company's advertising and so functions as an in-house agency. Among those firms that employ an advertising agency, the company's advertising department works closely with the agency. Some companies that manufacture a large number of products have even brand managers, who supervise the advertising and promotion of products. It is clear that, as we start the twenty-first century, advertising and business economics have become two sides of the same coin.

The advertising industry has now established associations that work to promote the industry and to raise the standards of advertising. The leading national advertising organizations include the *American Association of Advertising Agencies*, the *American Advertising Federation*, and the *Association of National Advertisers*. Two other important advertising organizations are the *Advertising Council* and the *National Advertising Review Board*. The former prepares public service ads, such as those that promote highway safety and energy conservation; the latter fosters self-regulation of the advertising industry, evaluating complaints about deceptive advertisements. If the council judges an advertisement to be false or misleading, it asks the advertiser to discontinue it. Most governments in industrialized countries, moreover, have laws designed to protect consumers from deceptive advertising. They also have regulations that prohibit certain kinds of advertising. For example, a federal law in the United States currently bans cigarette advertising on radio and television. But the Supreme Court of the United States has ruled that advertising and the advertising industry have some protection under the First Amendment to the United States Constitution. Thus, regulations concerning advertising must be no more restrictive than necessary to accomplish the goals of state and federal governments.

Laws on advertising differ in other parts of the world. In Australia, for example, most ads must be produced locally. China charges higher rates for foreign advertisers than for local companies or joint ventures. Agencies throughout the world support the *International Advertising Association*, which has headquarters in New York City. This organization works for truth in advertising, the protection of commercial speech, and improvements in the quality of media research.

The majority of jobs in advertising require a college education or special training. Approximately 30 colleges and universities in the United States offer major programs in the field of advertising. People with education in the liberal arts, journalism, behavioral sciences, business, semiotics, or commercial art may also find employment in the advertising industry. Information about careers in advertising are obtainable from the *American Advertising Federation* in Washington, DC, and from the *American Association of Advertising Agencies* in New York City.

4.2.2 Promoting consumerism

In our view, there is little doubt that the goal of the advertising industry is to promote consumerism, not just to enhance product recognizability. This is accomplished by essentially semiotic means - product naming, positioning, textuality, etc. - as we have seen throughout this textbook. Because the promotion is based on images (signs), it is highly effective. Day in and day out these fragmented images of life are bound to influence our overall view that reality is illusory, surreal as in the *Coco* or the *Versus* ads discussed in the previous chapter. Ultimately, we are led to form the view that human actions are a montage of disconnected images, desires, feelings, etc.

Traditionally, the religious forms of discourse - gospels, catechisms, sacred books, etc. - have always had, as one of their intents, the promulgation of the "good news" about the origin, development, and destiny of humanity. This is in fact the meaning of the word *gos-*

pel. Today, the good news, as Bachand (1992: 6) aptly claims, "is being announced by advertisers." Advertising now constitutes a form of discourse that celebrates consumption; it is the liturgy of consumerism. But this new catechism has no "divine author" with meaningful "answers to life." Its discourse categories merely announce that: "If you buy this or that, then you will be eternally young, sexy, happy, etc." No wonder, then, that mythic-religious themes - recall the mythic imagery implicit in the subtexts of the ads examined in previous chapters - pervade modern advertising. What is implicit in the advertising discourse is consumerist prophecy - a contemporary replacement of eschatological prophecy that once proclaimed the immanence of the afterlife in the present world. As Bachand (1992: 7) eloquently puts it: "The product literally seems like a creation emerging from the depths of formless matter to provide endless satisfaction."

As Spitzer (1979) has noted, it is ironic to contemplate that traditional Protestantism may have been the motivating force behind advertising's evolution and installment, since it has always encouraged the accumulation of goods in the world. As a consequence, it has unwittingly legitimized the contemporary discourse of advertising. The advertiser has, in a basic social sense, taken over the role of the preacher, promulgating the good news and the constant need to improve oneself. As Bachand (1992: 7) states: "There is a sermon in each advertisement; and all advertisers devote themselves to proclaiming their faith and the means of attaining paradise on earth through consumption and, in the meantime, through communication."

How did this all come about? Nietzsche's nihilistic prediction that "God was dead" meant, of course, that everything in human belief systems, including religious beliefs, can be seen by the reflective mind to be no more than constructions of that very mind. By the early part of the twentieth century the view that history had a purpose which was "narrated," so to speak, by a divine source (as, for example, in the Western Bible) was coming increasingly under attack. At mid-century, Western society was starting to become increasingly more "deconstructive," i.e. more inclined to take apart the structures - moral, social, and mental - that had been shaped by this narrative. By the 1960s, Western society had become fully entangled in a "postmodern" frame of mind, believing more and more that human beings fulfill no particular purpose for being alive, that life is a meaningless collage of actions on a relentless course leading back to nothingness.

Now, not everyone in our culture thinks in this way. There are many who, as a matter of fact, react against this kind of outlook. But it is becoming symptomatic of increasingly larger sectors of the culture. And, in our view, advertising has become the discourse style that reflects this cultural "symptomatology." Image-making has now become fully externalized in the form of products manipulated by media specialists. Television and advertising have become the postmodern mind's imagination and language. But the advertiser's imagination and his or her language typically fail to make a distinction between imagery and information on the one side, and true knowledge and wisdom on the other.

Many times this image-making promotes representations that are stereotypical. One of these was the portrayal of men as helpless slobs - a representational strategy that characterized ads and commercials throughout the 1990s and early twenty-first century. Take, for example, the Campbell's soup commercial of 2001 that painted the picture of a cozy family supper, where the kids thanked the mother profusely for the mouth-watering meal - with a background voice making it obvious that such a meal was so simple to make that "even dad" could make it (implying that men are fumbling ignoramuses).

4.2.3 Advertising as art

Advertising has become a kind of cultural *meta-language*, synthesizing verbal and nonverbal elements into a "compressed" textuality that sends out its message instantly, effortlessly, sensorially. As discussed previously, the magazine ad, for instance, can be viewed as contemporary *art* form, given that art of any type is a code-based form of representation that converts sense and feeling structures into signifying cultural texts. Magazine advertising is psychologically powerful because it combines the visual mode of representation (as do the fine arts) with the verbal one (as do the literary arts). As Henri Lefebvre (1968: 202-203) has put it, advertising has become the "poetry" of contemporary society, seizing "art and literature, with all available signifiers and vacant signifieds." As Bachand (1992: 3) also observes, since "ordinary" people today do not engage in "serious" reading or philosophical contemplation by and large, it should come as little surprise to find that advertising has come forward to provide "an opportunity for varied aesthetic experience." This is why the writer Georges Jean (1966: 82) remarked a few decades ago that advertising has come forward to fill the "need for poetry which exists in every human being."

Bachand (1992: 3) puts this whole line of criticism in perspective as follows:

> Thus advertising reinterprets the elements of semiological heritage in its own way, while taking modern sensibilities into account. It combines and transforms the processes and content of communication and thus participates in the updating and revival of the classical forms of expression.

No wonder, then, that advertising is being acknowledged as art more and more; having even its own prize category at the Cannes film festival. Although we may superciliously be inclined to condemn its objectives, as an aesthetic-inducing experience we invariably enjoy it. Advertisements convince, please, and seduce. Advertising works aesthetically. And advertising art is adaptive, constantly seeking out new forms of expression reflecting fluctuations in social trends and values. Not only, but its forms have even been adapted and coopted by mainstream artists and writers. Some pages of the contemporary writer Jean Marie Gustave Le Clézio, for instance, reveal an amalgam of traditional literary expression and advertising styles and forms. As Bachand (1992: 6) states, in this way "a dialectic of recuperation and diversion is developed, and through it the different semiotic systems that constitute the prevailing social imagination are refracted."

But there is a fundamental difference between the great works of art that all cultures identify as "saying something" about life and advertising. The goal of the great artists has always been to imbue our universal human experience with meaning and sense of purpose. The great works of visual art, the great dramas, the great music of *all* cultures, not just the Western one, are meant to transform the experience of human feelings and events into memorable works that transcend time and culture. Advertising, on the other hand, communicates nothing of any lasting or profound value, but trendy, "cool" attitudes and images. This new artistic vernacular constitutes a means aimed at grabbing the attention of a generation of individuals with seemingly reduced attention spans. Advertising is the art of the trivial, quickly becoming all too familiar and boring.

4.3 The semiotic purview

The essence of semiotic method lies in identifying how signs are used to represent something. In the case of advertising that something is usually a need, a desire, etc. As a form of representation and social communication, advertising is, as we have seen, a sign-based process, i.e. a process that entails signification. Knowing which signifiers to use to convey advertising messages is the essence of the trade of advertising. Advertising is all about *signification* through skillful *representation*. In line with the fundamental *law* of the marketing alluded to in the opening chapter (1.2.3), it is a form of text-making that is geared towards enhancing the salability of a product or service by associating it with some desire or need through some culturally-significant *representational* process. It is not important that one or the other *interpretation* of an ad is the correct one, as we have seen; what counts is that various interpretations are possible in the first place. The more interpretations there are, the more likely the effectiveness of the ad.

4.3.1 The effects of advertising

Even though we absorb the messages transmitted constantly by ads and commercials, and although these may have some unconscious effects on our behavior, we accept media images only if they suit our already-established preferences. If we complain about the shallowness of our television and advertising culture, we really have no one to blame but ourselves.

It is true, however, that advertising has probably contributed significantly to creating a desire for the lifestyles it portrays in other parts of the world. When asked about the stunning defeat of communism in eastern Europe, the Polish leader Lech Walesa was reported by the newspapers as saying that it all came from the television set, implying that television undermined the stability of the communist world's relatively poor and largely sheltered lifestyle with images of consumer delights seen in western programs and commercials. Different cultures have indeed been reshaped to the form and contents of television's textuality. Marshall McLuhan's phrase of the "global village" is still an appropriate one - television and advertising have shrunk the world and diminished the interval between thought and action.

Demographic surveys now show consistently that people spend more time in front of television sets than they do working, that watching TV is bringing about a gradual decline in reading, that television's textuality is leading to the demise of the nation state concept as ideas and images cross national boundaries daily through television channels. When Gutenberg invented movable type to print the Bible, he initiated a veritable revolution in human mental evolution and culture by making ideas readily available to a larger population. Television and advertising have triggered the twentieth century's own "Gutenberg revolution." But rather than homogenizing the world, it is our view that human diversity and ingenuity will lead to a greater variety in television programming and advertising and, therefore, in social textuality. Our craving for variety is perhaps what gives us an edge in the struggle for survival in a constantly changing world.

Advertising has been good for economics. Although some economists believe that a large amount of the money spent on advertising is wasted, arguing that much of it simply leads consumers to switch from one brand of a product to another brand, thus having no positive effect on the overall economy, there is no doubt that, without it, we would be living in a vastly different economic universe, not to mention psychological one. For one thing, it is the fuel for the economic engine that runs the mass media and mass entertainment industries. Advertising pays all the costs of commercial television and radio, for instance, providing everyone with free entertainment and news programs, even though many people may be irritated by commercial interruptions. Advertising also pays three-fourths of the costs of newspapers and magazines. Without advertising, readers would have to pay a higher price for newspapers and magazines, and many of the publications would go out of business. Because the mass media depend on advertising to stay in business, some social critics question whether advertisers control the media. They maintain that dependence on advertising lowers the quality of TV programming. In order to sell advertising time at high prices, TV networks try to attract the largest possible audience. Critics argue that the stations therefore broadcast too many general entertainment programs and not enough informational and cultural programs.

Advertising has extended its reach into virtually all domains of social interaction. For example, advertisements are now seen in movie theaters and on videotapes and DVDs prior to the featured movie. Ads appear on ski lift towers, and in high school classroom news programming. In supermarkets, shoppers may be exposed to in-store radio, grocery carts with miniature billboards or video screens, and TV sets with programs or commercials in the checkout line. Realizing that the same kinds of persuasive techniques could be used to promote candidates, in 1952 even politics got into the "advertising game," when Dwight D. Eisenhower successfully ran for the United States presidency, with the help of advertising executives, who directed Eisenhower's presidential campaign. No wonder, then, that, since 1952, advertising has played an increasingly important role in political campaigns, with TV spot announcements having become a major strategy of campaigns for public offices at all levels of government. "It pays to advertise," has become the aphorism of the contemporary world.

Advertising is, in effect, a modern-day form of magic. The manufacturers of such products as gasoline and headache remedies, for instance, boast of new, secret ingredients - in the same way that magicians would use secret charms, spells, and rituals in seeking or pretending to cause or control events, or govern certain natural or supernatural forces. Like magic, advertising promises implicitly to produce marvelous effects through supernatural or occult powers. Advertisements may indirectly suggest that a mouthwash or a toothpaste will magically transform an unpopular person into a popular one. Consumers will buy these for the magical qualities suggested by such advertising, without critical thought. As we have seen throughout this textbook, advertisers use suggestion in many ways. No advertiser would dare guarantee that a person will become popular by using a certain product. But the advertisements may strongly suggest this result.

The greatest critique of advertising was leveled, as we have discussed throughout this manual, by the semiotician Roland Barthes, who claimed that it fostered a culture of neomania, a state of groupthink that artfully propels people to buy products they do not need or want. More recently, critics have accused advertising of generating an unhealthy hedonistic and Epicurean worldview. Lifestyle advertising in particular is seen as mirroring how contemporary humans in the mass perceive reality - as a collage of images that promote physical and social desires. The subtext of advertising is criticized for conveying the message that the only meaningful thing to life is enjoyment, prestige, security, attractiveness, etc. In the past, these would have been considered either sins or manifestations of vanity. Advertising is also trenchantly criticized for providing messages of assurance that consumption in itself can solve all human problems - perhaps even prolong life indefinitely and thus conquering death. Viewing the world through a television commercial or through magazine ads is bound, eventually, to transform the human view of the real world into a gaze that interprets it as if it were a TV program or a scene in an ad. Day in and day out advertising's fragmented images of life are bound to influence our overall view that reality is illusory and surreal - satisfying desires is the only thing that counts.

The language of advertising has also had an effect on the language of ordinary communication. Advertising language reduces thoughts to formulas, stock phrases, jingles, slogans. Its conceptual system is not tied to a larger social, religious, or philosophical grammar. It is instantaneous, geared to encapsulating fleeting images and condensed thoughts. Advertising now constitutes a form of discourse that celebrates consumption; it is the liturgy of consumerism. But this new catechism has no "divine author" with meaningful "answers to life."

Advertising has also developed its own historiography. Retro ads of the late 1990s, for instance, constituted works of historical self-reference. With computer techniques, images from 1950s commercials are incorporated into modern-day TV commercials, conveying a feeling for the supposedly simple, secure, good life of that era, and, at the same time, documenting the history of advertising. Providing a sense of order through historical continuity and recapitulated images, retro advertising is just one way in which advertisers adapt to change and need.

4.3.2 Final reflections

Even though we absorb the messages transmitted constantly by ads and commercials, and although these may have some unconscious effects on our behavior, we accept media images only if they suit our already-established preferences. If we complain about the shallowness of our television and advertising culture, we really have no one to blame but ourselves.

Thus, at the risk of sounding élitist, we believe that advertising will never be able to replace the traditional forms of artistic expression. These document humanity's search for spiritual meaning; their subtexts are open-ended and profound. Advertising, on the other hand, exploits our need for meaning trivially to enhance sales of a product. Many critics refer to the effects of advertising as *reification*, the process of encouraging people to identify their desires and needs with objects that can be bought and sold. We agree. Advertising seems no more just to advertise products, but to promote a way of life through reification. But we must not forget, as Leiss, Kline and Jhally (1990: 33) remind us, that: "Objections directed at advertisements, the industry, and its alleged social impacts are often indirect attacks on the so-called materialistic ethos of industrial society, or on capitalism in general as a social system; these are critiques of society masquerading as critiques of advertising."

The answer to the dilemma of advertising is not to be found in censorship or in any form of state control of media . Even if it were possible in a consumerist culture to control the contents of advertising, this would invariably prove to be counterproductive. The answer is, in our view, to become aware of the subtexts that ads and commercials generate with the help of semiotic analysis. When the human mind is aware of the hidden codes in texts, it will be better able to fend off the undesirable effects that such texts may cause. Semiotics can help to demystify advertising creativity.

As we have attempted to show in this book, advertisements generate a truly interesting and rich array of connotations. These can be deciphered by analyzing the iconic and verbal cues of the surface ad text semiotically. Once the subtext has been decoded, the appeal of the ad seems to vanish, even in the case of highly connotative ads like the *Chanel* ones.

Aware that advertising has become a threat to spiritual and ecological survival, there has been a considerable backlash against the whole capitalistic, corporate culture that it serves in the last few years. In *Culture Jam* (2000), for instance, the Canadian activist Kalle Lasn makes a persuasive case against the globalization of consumerist culture. As a leading voice in the so-called "culture jamming" movement, Lasn (who is also the founder of *Adbusters* magazine, which satirizes ads and commercials) is at the front of a new youth movement that decries the mindless consumerism of modern society, at the cost of spiritual and ecological disaster.

But this resistance movement to the corporate homogenization of global culture does not provide an alternative. The corporate world has replaced the religious order of medieval times. But at least the former has not taken the drastic measures that the religious order did in attempting to preserve is control of society. There are no capitalist Inquistions. After all, it is up to the individual in a consumerist culture to simply say "No." There is nothing more effective, in our view, than personal choice. This is one of the main reasons why we wrote this book in the first place. Even the widespread use of cosmetics has been useful socially, as Kathy Peiss (1998) has recently intimated, because it liberated women to express their sexuality - something that religious cultures have always tended to strictly forbid. The founders and early leaders of the "cosmetic movement" were simple women - Elizabeth Arden (1884-1966), a Canadian, was the daughter of poor tenant farmers, Helena Rubinstein (1870–1965), was born of poor Jewish parents in Poland, and Madam C. J. Walker (1867-1919) was born to former slaves in Louisiana. While it is true that advertising has preyed on social fears associated with "bad complexions," "aging," etc. it has nevertheless allowed women to assert their right to emphasize their sexuality, not conceal it.

In the end, it may be true that advertising may be reshaping the world in more ways than we might think. As we look at people shopping, at parties, driving down the road, sitting at outdoor cafés sipping coffee, etc. we cannot help but see in their bodily schemas, in the way they wear their clothes, in the discourse they generate, a re-enactment of many of the images and scenes created by advertisers. We witnessed a striking example of this a few years ago when we attended a party of young upscale professionals. At a certain point during the evening, we saw an interactional scene that reminded us of a beer commercial that was popular on television at the time. The young men and women were posturing towards each other in ways that were almost identical to those of the actors in the television commercial. A culture mediated so pervasively by advertising images is asking for trouble. What Kubey and Csikszentmihalyi (1990: 199) have to say about the psychosocial effects of television applies, in our view, as well to advertising:

> Because consciousness is necessarily formed by exposure to information, media fare helps define what our most important and salient goals should be. Being an intimate part of the consumer society, television tells us that a worthwhile life is measured in terms of how many desirable material objects we get to own, and how many pleasures we get to feel. To achieve such goals complex skills are unnecessary. Even though some people spend a great deal of attention in trying to find bargains, in monitoring prices and sales, in developing culinary taste and fashion sense, in keeping abreast of new models and new gadgets, for the most part consumption does not require much disciplined effort and therefore does not produce psychological growth.

The answer to the dilemma of advertising is, in our view, to become aware of the subtexts that brands, logos, ads, and commercials generate with the help of semiotic analysis. When the human mind is aware of the hidden codes in texts, it will be better able to fend off the undesirable effects that such codes may cause. As Drummond (1991: 7) has put it, semiotics can help to demystify advertising creativity and make "the process of meaning creation more accessible."

Appendix
Exercises for classroom or personal study use

Chapter I

1.1 Suggest strategies for enhancing product recognizability.

1.2 What aspects of modern-day large businesses entail *propaganda, publicity,* and *public relations*, in addition to *advertising* and/or *marketing*?

1.3 What ways, other than those mentioned in this chapter, can ensure that a product will "generate new demand" for a product and, thus, ensconce neomania?

1.4 Create a new campaign for *Absolut Vodka* that is similar to the one described in this chapter.

1.5 What signifieds are associated with the following product names?

> *IBM*
> *Macintosh*
> *Gucci*
> *Camel cigarettes*
> *Marlboro cigarettes*
> *Timex*
> *Swatch*
> *Omega*
> *Sony*

1.6 Suggest ways of promoting high heel shoes with contemporary forms of advertising.

Chapter II

2.1 Identify and define the main strategies used for enhancing product recognizability.

2.2 Give a common brand name and trademark (if one exists) for each of the following products/services, identifying the system of connotations it evokes and what kind of textuality is used for it.

automobile
cat food
cigarettes
detergent
dog food
insurance company
men's cologne
men's watch
pain tablet
women's perfume
women's watch

2.3 Invent either an iconic, indexical, or symbolic brand name or logo for each type of new product/service.

appliance
automobile
bank
cereal
cigarette
courier
eyeglasses
furniture
hotel
resort
travel service

2.4 Create signification systems with brand names, logos, and textualities for the following new product/service lines:

beer
chocolate bar
cigarettes
courier
eyeglasses
family van
furniture
men's pants
pasta
wine
women's pants

2.5 Suggest media for establishing product recognizability and image of the above new products/services.

2.6 Describe ad campaigns you would design for the following new products:

> *a new automobile*
> *a new computer*
> *a new soft drink*
> *a new cosmetic*

2.7 What kinds of lifestyle forms are advertisers currently coopting? Give specific examples.

2.8 Come up with brand names and logos for each of the following new products. Explain the rationale used:

> *automobile*
> *watch*
> *athletic shoes*
> *oven cleanser*
> *lipstick*
> *shaving lotion*
> *stereo system*

Chapter III

3.1 Collect several print ads of lifestyle products. Then for each one identify:

> *their verbal signifiers*
> *their nonverbal signifiers*
> *their connotative chains*
> *their subtexts*
> *their intertexts*

3.2 Design ads for any lifestyle product based on the following connotative chains: i.e. for each chain construct an ad that renders it at a surface level - (1) identify the product; (2) give it a brand name; (3) design an ad for it:

> *red = passion = sexuality = heat = etc.*
> *smile = friendliness = trust = neighborliness = etc.*
> *twilight = suspension of belief = eerieness = occultism = etc.*

white = beauty = illumination = innocence = cleanliness = etc.

3.3 Indicate which of the following products/services will, probably, have a low, mid, or high connotative index in its textuality:

beer
chocolate bar
cigarette
classified ad
courier
eyeglasses
family van
furniture
insurance
men's pants
pasta
real estate
wine
women's pants

3.4 Invent slogans (jingles without music) for the following products:

appliance
bank
beer
chocolate bar
cigarette
courier
eyeglasses
family van
furniture
hotel
insurance
men's pants
pasta
real estate
resort
travel service
wine
women's pants

3.5 Using the notion of connotative index:

- First carry out an analysis of 10 ads for different lifestyle products (taken from different magazines).

- Then, ask a group of people (e.g. other students in the class) what each ad means to them.

- On that basis, assign a connotative index to each ad (high, mid, low):

3.6 Suggest brand names, draw logos, and coin slogans or jingles for the following new products. Then provide the connotative chain(s) that you intend to generate with such strategies.

> *bra*
> *car*
> *cell phone*
> *cheese*
> *jeans*
> *laptop*
> *nail polish*
> *panty hose*
> *toothpaste*
> *toy*
> *wine*

3.7 Now design and create several ads and/or commercials (using video equipment) that will deliver the signification system you have established for each product.

Chapter IV

4.1 Using Case *1* as background, flesh out the product image of an automobile of your choice with a group of students in the class. Use the following techniques:

> *Imaginary world*
> *Portrait chinois*
> *Picture association*
> *Slogan*

4.2 Identify the primary connotative chains generated by the automobile. What would your recommendation be to the manufacturer who wishes to change its image?

4.3 Using Case 2 as background, determine whether co-branding a popular donut shop chain with a cineplex chain would be additive or subtractive. Use real brands.

4.4 Using the notion of semantic differential, set-up various scales to flesh out the connotations of well-known brands of the following products or services:

> *automobile*
> *insurance company*
> *perfume*
> *toothpaste*

4.5 You are given the task of redefining certain well-known products or services. You are to do this by changing the brand name and logo (if one exists) of each product or service, identifying the new system of connotations this is supposed to evoke and what kind of new textuality is to be used for it.

> *American Express (credit card)*
> *Bayer (aspirin)*
> *Burger King (restaurant)*
> *Cadillac (automobile)*
> *Camels (cigarettes)*
> *Drakkar Noir (cologne)*
> *Fedex (courier)*
> *Fox Network (TV network)*
> *Kellog's (cereal)*
> *Kodak (photography)*
> *Macintosh (computer)*
> *Marlboro (cigarettes)*
> *Marriott (hotel chain)*
> *Memorex (cassette tape)*
> *Poison (perfume)*
> *Purina Dog Chow*
> *Rémy Martin (cognac)*
> *Sunlight (detergent)*
> *Timex (watch)*
> *Tylenol (pain killer)*
> *Versus (cologne)*
> *Wendy's (restaurant)*

4.6 Using Case 1 as background, flesh out the product image of *Marlboro* cigarettes in contrast with *Camel's* cigarettes with a group of students in the class.

Glossary of technical terms

A

advertising	any type or form of public announcement designed to promote the sale of specific commodities or services
aesthesia	the ability to experience sensation; in art appreciation it refers to the fact that the senses and feelings are stimulated by the art form
alliteration	the repetition of the initial consonant sounds or phonetic features of words
anchorage	Roland Barthes' notion that visual images in advertisements are polysemous (having many meanings) which are, however, anchored to particular meaning domains by specific interpreters

B

brand image	the creation of a personality for a product: i.e. the intentional creation of a product's name, packaging, price, and advertising style in order to create a recognizable personality for the product that is meant to appeal to specific consumers
brand name	name given to a product

C

channel	the physical means by which a signal or message is transmitted
code	the system in which signs are organized and which determines how they relate to each other in meaningful texts
cognitive style	the particular way in which information and knowledge are processed (understood and memorized)
communication	social interaction through messages; the production and exchange of messages and meanings; the use of specific modes and media of sign-making to transmit feeling-states and messages

conceptual metaphor	the generalized metaphorical formula that defines a specific abstraction (*love is a sweet taste*)
connotation	the extended or secondary meaning of a sign; the symbolic or mythic meaning of a certain signifier (word, image, etc.)
connotative chain	a chain of connotations associated with a product as generated by ads and commercials about the product, by the brand name used, etc.
connotative index	the degree of connotation associated with a product; a measure of the number of connotations generated by an ad, commercial, brand name, etc.
consumer advertising	advertising directed toward the promotion of some product
context	the situation - physical, psychological, and/or social - in which a sign or text is used or occurs, or to which it refers
cultural modeling	the association of various source domains with one target domain, producing an overall, or culture-specific model, of the target domain
culture	the system of daily living that is held together by a signifying order (signs, codes, texts, connective forms)

D

decoding	the process of deciphering the message inherent in a brand name, ad text, etc.
denotation	the primary meaning of a sign
diachronic	the historical dimension of signs

E

encoding	the process of putting a message together in terms of a specific code or codes

F

fetish	an object that is believed to have magical or spiritual powers, or which can cause sexual arousal

G

ground	the part of a metaphor that generates its meaning
Gutenberg Galaxy	term coined by Marshall McLuhan to characterize the radical new social order ushered in by the invention of the printing press

H

hermeneutics	the science or art of interpretation of texts

I

icon	a sign that has a direct (nonarbitrary) connection to a referent
iconicity	the process of representing referents with iconic forms
Id	Sigmund Freud's term for the unconscious part of the psyche actuated by fundamental impulses toward fulfilling instinctual needs
image	representation of a product or service in order to enhance its value aesthetically, socially, etc.
image schema	mental impression of locations, movements, shapes, etc.
index	a sign that has an existential connection to a referent (indicating that something or someone is located somewhere)
indexicality	the process of representing referents with indexical signs
intercodality	the interconnection of various codes (linguistic, musical, visual, etc.) in the making of ad texts
interpretant	the process of adapting a sign's meaning to personal and social experience
intertextuality	the allusion within a text to some other text that the interpreter/receiver would have access to or knowledge of

J

jingle	an easy rhythmic and simple repetition of sound, etc., as in poetry and music

L

logo	the distinctive company signature, trademark, colophon, motto, newspaper nameplate, etc.

M

marketing	the business of positioning goods and services
medium	the technical or physical means by which a message is transmitted
message	any meaningful text produced with signs belonging to a specific code (or codes)
metaphor	the signifying process by which two signifying domains *(A, B)* are connected *(A is B)* explicitly or implicitly
metonymy	the signifying process by which an entity is used to refer to another that is related to it
myth	any story or narrative that aims to explain the origin of something
mythology	the set of mythic connotations associated with a product's name, or generated by an ad or commercial

N

name	a sign that identifies a human being or, by connotative extension, an animal, an object (such as a commercial product), and event (such as a hurricane)
narrative	something narrated, told or written, such as an account, story, tale, and even scientific theory
narrative mode	the use of narrativity as the cognitive means by which something is conceptualized and then expressed - "narrated" - in verbal and/or nonverbal ways
narrativity	the innate human capacity to produce and comprehend narratives

O

object	a synonym for referent or signified; what is referred to in signification

onomatopoeia	the iconic feature of words by which they represent a referent through the simulation of one or several of its audio-oral features (*drip, boom*, etc.)
opposition	the process by which signs are differentiated through a minimal change in their forms (signifiers)

P

paradigmaticity	a differentiation property of signs
parallelism	the repetition of linguistic patterns (sentences, phrases, etc.)
percept	a unit of perception (a stimulus that has been received and recognized); an immediate unit of knowing derived from sensation or feeling
positioning	the placing or marketing of a product for the right people
propaganda	any systematic dissemination of doctrines, views, etc. reflecting specific interests and ideologies (political, social, and so on)
public relations	the activities and techniques used by organizations and/or individuals to establish favorable attitudes and responses in their behalf on the part of the general public or of special groups
publicity	the craft of disseminating any information that concerns a person, group, event, or product through some form of public media

R

receiver	the one who decodes a message; the target of an ad, ad campaign, commercial, etc.
referent	what is referred to by a sign (any object, being, idea, or event in the world)
representation	the process of ascribing a form to some referent
rhetoric	the study of the techniques used in all kinds of discourses, from common conversation to poetry

S

semantic differential	the technique used in semiotics for fleshing our connotations from a product's image through contrasting scales

semiology	Ferdinand de Saussure's term for the study of signs, now restricted, by and large, to the study of verbal signs
semiosis	the comprehension and production of signs
semiotics	the science or doctrine that studies signs
sender	the transmitter of a message
sense ratio	the level at which one of the senses is activated during the encoding and decoding of forms
sign	something that stands for something (someone) else in some capacity
signification	the relation that holds between a sign and its referent
signification system	system of meanings created for a product through the creation of a brand name, a logo, and appropriate forms of advertising
signified	that part of a sign that is referred to (the referent); also called image, object, or concept
signifier	that part of a sign that does the referring; the physical part of a sign
signifying order	the interconnected system of signs, texts, codes, etc. that constitute a culture
slogan	a catchword or catch phrase used to advertise a product
source domain	the set of vehicles (concrete forms) that is used to deliver the meaning of an abstract concept
structuralism	the approach in semiotics that views signs as reflexes of intellectual and emotional structures
structure	any repeatable or predictable aspect of meaning systems
structure	any repeatable or predictable aspect of signs, codes, and messages
subtext	a concealed system of connotative meanings within an ad text
symbol	a sign that has an arbitrary (conventional) connection with a referent
symbolicity	the process of representing referents with symbolic forms
symbolism	symbolic meaning in general
synchronic	the study of signs as the are at a specific point in time (usually the present)

synesthesia	the evocation of one sense modality (e.g. vision) by means of some other (e.g. hearing); the juxtaposition of sense modalities (e.g. *loud colors*)
syntagmatic	the structural relation by which signs are combined in code-dependent ways

T

target domain	what a conceptual metaphor is about (the abstract concept that is metaphorized)
tautology	a statement that is meaningless but enunciated as necessarily true
tenor	the subject of a metaphor; a synonym for topic
text	the actual message with its particular form and contents
textuality	the complex of product meanings embedded into ads and commercials
topic	the subject of a metaphor (a synonym for tenor)
trade advertising	advertising that is directed toward dealers and professionals through appropriate trade publications and media
trope	a figure of speech; figurative language generally

V

vehicle	the part of a metaphor to which a tenor is connected; the part that makes a concrete statement about the tenor

Works cited and general bibliography

Aaker, D. A.

1996   *Building Strong Brands*. New York: The Free Press.

Abercrombie, N.

1996   *Television and Society*. Cambridge: Polity Press.

Abruzzese, Alberto

1988   *Metafore della pubblicità*. Genova: Costa & Nolan.

Ackerman, Frank

1997   *The History of Consumer Society*. Washington, DC: Island Press.

Adatto, K.

1993   *Picture Perfect: The Art and Artifice of Public Image Making*. New York: Basic Books.

Albion, M. and P. Farris

1981   *The Advertising Controversy*. Boston: Auburn House.

Alexander, M. M. Burt, and A. Collinson

1995   Big talk, small talk: BTS strategic use of semiotics in planning and current advertising. *Journal of Market Research* 37: 91-102.

Alsted, C. and H. H. Larsen

1991   Choosing complexity of signs in ads. *Marketing Signs* 10: 1-14.

Anderson, M.

1984   *Madison Avenue in Asia: Politics and Transnational Advertising*. Cranbury, N. J.: Associated University Presses.

Anderson, W. T.

1992   *Reality Isn't What It Used to Be*. San Francisco: Harper Collins.

Andren, G. L., L. Ericsson, R. Ohlsson, and T. Tännsjö

1978   *Rhetoric and Ideology in Advertising*. Stockholm: AB Grafiska.

Argyle, Michael

1988   *Bodily Communication*. New York: Methuen.

Arnheim, Rudolf

1969   *Visual Thinking*. Berkeley: University of California Press.

Asch, Solomon

1950   On the use of metaphor in the description of persons. In: H. Werner (ed.), *On Expressive Language*, 86–94. Worcester: Clark University Press.

1958   The metaphor: A psychological inquiry. In: R. Tagiuri and L. Petrullo
        (eds.), *Person Perception and Interpersonal Behavior*, 28-42. Stan-
        ford: Stanford University Press.

Atwan, R.
1979   *Edsels, Luckies and Frigidaires: Advertising the American Way*. New
        York: Dell.

Axtell, Roger E.
1991   *Gestures*. New York: John Wiley.

Bachand, Denis
1992   The art of (in) advertising: From poetry to prophecy. *Marketing Signs*
        13: 1-7.

Bal, Mieke
1985   *Narratology: Introduction to the Theory of the Narrative*. Toronto:
        University of Toronto Press.

Baldwin, H.
1989   *How to Create Effective TV Commercials*. Lincolnwood, Ill.: NTC
        Business Books.

Ballotta, F. and Franco Brigida
1982   *Radio e pubblicità*. Torino: Forma.

Barlow, Horace, Colin Blakemore, and Miranda Weston-Smith (eds.)
1990   *Images and Understanding*. Cambridge: Cambridge University Press.

Barnouw, E.
1978   *The Sponsor: Notes on a Modern Potentate*. Oxford: Oxford Univer-
        sity Press.

Barthel, Diane
1988   *Putting on Appearances: Gender and Advertising*. Philadelphia:
        Temple University Press.

Barthes, Roland
1957   *Mythologies*. Paris: Seuil.
1964   *Éléments de sémiologie*. Paris: Seuil.
1967   *Système de la mode*. Paris: Seuil.
1970   *S/Z*, trans. by R. Miller. New York: Hill and Wang
1977   *Image-Music-Text*. London: Fontana.

Bauman, Z.
1992   *Intimations of Postmodernity*. London: Routledge.

Beasley, Ron, Marcel Danesi, and Paul Perron

2000   *Signs for Sale: An Outline of Semiotic Analysis for Advertisers and Marketers.* Ottawa: Legas Press.

Beaudrillard, Jean

1981   *For a Critique of the Political Economy of the Sign.* St. Louis: Telos Press.

Bell, S.

1990   Semiotics and advertising research: A Case Study. *Marketing Signs* 8: 1-6.

Bendinger, B.

1988   *The Copy Workshop Workbook.* Chicago: The Copy Workshop.

Berger, Arthur A.

1996   *Manufacturing Desire: Media, Popular Culture, and Everyday Life.* New Brunswick, NJ : Transaction Publishers.

2000   *Ads, Fads, and Consumer Culture: Advertising's Impact on American Character and Society.* Lanham: Rowman & Littlefield.

Berger, John

1972   *Ways of Seeing.* Harmondsworth: Penguin.

Berman, Neil (ed.)

1998   *The Mass Media: Opposing Viewpoints.* San Diego: Greenhaven Press.

Bernardelli, Andrea (ed.)

1997   *The Concept of Intertextuality Thirty Years On: 1967-1997.* Special Issue of *Versus,* 77/78. Milano: Bompiani.

Bignell, Jonathan

1997   *Media Semiotics: An Introduction.* Manchester: Manchester University Press.

Black, Max

1962   *Models and Metaphors.* Ithaca: Cornell University Press.

Bouissac, Paul (ed.)

1986   *Iconicity: Essays on the Nature of Culture.* Tübingen: Stauffenberg.

Branston, G. and R. Stafford

1999   *The Media Student's Book.* London: Routledge.

Brierley, S.

1995   *The Advertising Handbook.* London: Routledge.

Brigida, F., L. Francia, and L. Di Vesme
   1993   *La pubblicità in Italia.* Milano: Lupetti.
Briggs, A. and Paul Cobley (eds.)
   1998   *The Media: An Introduction.* Harlow: Longman.
Bühler, Karl
   1934   *Sprachtheorie: Die Darstellungsfunktion der Sprache.* Jena: Fischer.
   1951 [1908]   On thought connection. In: D. Rapaport (ed.), *Organization and Pathology of Thought*, 81-92. New York: Columbia University Press.
Campbell, Joseph
   1969   *Primitive Mythology.* Harmondsworth: Penguin.
Cashmore, E.
   1994   *And There Was Television.* London: Routledge.
Cherwitz, Richard and James Hikins
   1986   *Communication and Knowledge: An Investigation in Rhetorical Epistemology.* Columbia: University of South Carolina Press.
Clarke, D. S.
   1987   *Principles of Semiotic.* London: Routledge and Kegan.
Classen, C.
   1993   *Worlds of Sense: Exploring the Senses in History and across Cultures.* London: Routledge.
Classen, C., D. Howes, and A. Synnott
   1994   *Aroma: The Cultural History of Smell.* London: Routledge.
Cleveland, C. E.
   1986   Semiotics: Determining what the advertising message means to the audience. In: J. Olson and K. Sentis (eds.), *Advertising and Consumer Psychology*, Vol. 3, 227–241. New York: Praeger.
Colton, Helen
   1983   *The Gift of Touch.* New York: Putnam.
Connor, M. K.
   1995   *Cool: Understanding Black Manhood in America.* New York: Crown.
Courtenoy, A. E. and T. W. Whipple
   1983   *Sex Stereotyping in Advertising.* Lexington, Mass.: Lexington Books.
Cox, Maureen
   1992   *Children's Drawings.* Harmondsworth: Penguin.

Craik, J.

    1993   *The Face of Fashion: Cultural Studies in Fashion*. London: Routledge.

Crispin Miller, Mark

    1988   *Boxed In: The Culture of TV*. Evanston: Northwestern University Press.

Czerniawski, Richard D. and Michael W. Maloney

    1999   *Creating Brand Loyalty*. New York: Amacom.

Danesi, Marcel

    1994   *Cool: The Signs and Meanings of Adolescence*. Toronto: University of Toronto Press.

    1998   Gender assignment, markedness, and indexicality: Results of a pilot study. *Semiotica* 121 (3/4): 213-239.

    1999   *Of Cigarettes, High Heels, and Other Interesting Things*. New York: St. Martin's.

Danesi, Marcel and Paul Perron

    1999   *Analyzing Cultures*. Bloomington: Indiana University Press.

Danna, Sammy R.

    1992   *Advertising and Popular Culture: Studies in Variety and Versatility*. Bowling Green, Ohio: Bowling Green State University Popular Press.

Davies, R.

    1989   *How to Read Faces*. Woolnough: Aquarian.

Davis, F.

    1992   *Fashion, Culture, and Identity*. Chicago: University of Chicago Press.

Deely, John

    1990   *Basics of Semiotics*. Bloomington: Indiana University Press.

Dingena, Marian

    1994   *The Creation of Meaning in Advertising Interaction of Figurative Advertising and Individual Differences in Processing Styles*. Amsterdam: Thesis Publishers.

Docker, J.

    1994   *Postmodernism and Popular Culture: A Cultural History*. Cambridge: Cambridge University Press.

Douglas, S. J.

    1994   *Where the Girls Are: Growing Up Female with the Mass Media*. New York: Times.

Driver, J. C. and G. R. Foxall
  1984   *Advertising Policy and Practice.* New York: Holt, Rinehart and Winston.

Drummond, G.
  1991   An irresistible force: Semiotics in advertising practice. *Marketing Signs* 10: 1-7.

Dyer, Gillian
  1982   *Advertising as Communication.* London: Routledge.

Eco, Umberto
  1976   *A Theory of Semiotics.* Bloomington: Indiana University Press.
  1979   *The Role of the Reader: Explorations in the Semiotics of Texts.* Bloomington: Indiana University Press.
  1984   *Semiotics and the Philosophy of Language.* Bloomington: Indiana University Press.

Ekman, Paul
  1985   *Telling Lies.* New York: Norton.

Ekman, Paul and Walter Friesen
  1975   *Unmasking the Face.* Englewood Cliffs: Prentice-Hall.

Elliot, B.
  1962   *A History of English Advertising.* London: Batsford.

Ewen, Stuart
  1976   *Captains of Consciousness.* New York: McGraw-Hill.
  1988   *All Consuming Images.* New York: Basic.

Fabris, Giampaolo
  1992   *La pubblicità. Teorie e prassi.* Milano: Angeli.

Fisher, Helen E.
  1992   *Anatomy of Love.* New York: Norton.

Fleming, Dan
  1996   *Powerplay: Toys as Popular Culture.* Manchester: Manchester University Press.

Forceville, Charles
  1996   *Pictorial Metaphor in Advertising.* London: Routledge.

Foules, Jib
  1996   *Advertising and Popular Culture.* Thousand Oaks: Sage.

Fowles, L.

1976   *Mass Advertising as Social Forecast: A Method for Futures Research.* Westport: Greenwood Press.

Fox, S.

1984   *The Mirror Makers.* New York: William Morrow.

Fries, Peter H.

1993   Information flow in written advertising. In: J. E. Alatis (ed.), *Language, Communication, and Social Meaning*, 336-352. Washington, D. C.: Georgetown University Press.

Frith, Katherine Toland

1997   *Undressing the Ad: Reading Culture in Advertising.* New York: Peter Lang.

Frutiger, A.

1989   *Signs and Symbols.* New York: Van Nostrand.

Geiss, Michael L.

1982   *The Language of Television Advertising.* New York: Academic.

Gibbs, Raymond W.

1994   *The Poetics of Mind: Figurative Thought, Language, and Understanding.* Cambridge: Cambridge University Press.

Goatley, Andrew

1997   *The Language of Metaphors.* London: Routledge.

Goffman, Erving

1959   *The Presentation of Self in Everyday Life.* New York: Anchor.

1979   *Gender Advertisements.* New York: Harper and Row.

Goldman, Robert

1994   *Reading Ads Socially.* London: Routledge.

Goldman, Robert and Stephen Papson

1996   *Sign Wars: The Cluttered Landscape of Advertising.* New York: The Guilford Press.

Greimas, Algirdas J.

1987   *On Meaning: Selected Essays in Semiotic Theory*, trans. by P. Perron and F. Collins. Minneapolis: University of Minnesota Press.

Harris, Alan C.

1995   Absolutely a semiome: Visual and linguistic manipulation in print advertising. In: C. W. Spinks and John Deely (eds.), *Semiotics 1994*, 360-369. New York: Peter Lang.

Harris, R. and A. Seldon
   1962   *Advertising and the Public*. London: André Deutsch.

Hawkes, Terrence
   1977   *Structuralism and Semiotics*. Berkeley: University of California
           Press.

Hayakawa, S. I.
   1991   *Language in Thought and Action*, 5th ed. New York: Harcourt,
           Brace, Jovanovich.

Heighton, E. and D. Cunningham
   1976   *Advertising in the Broadcast Media*. Belmont: Wadsworth.

Heinberg, R.
   1989   *Memories and Visions of Paradise*. Los Angeles: J. P. Tarcher.

Hermerén, Lars
   1999   *English for Sale: A Study of the Language of Advertising*. Lund: Lund
           University Press.

Hindley, D. and G. Hindley
   1972   *Advertising in Victorian England*. London: Wayland.

Hine, Thomas
   1995   *The Total Package: The Secret History and Hidden Meanings of
           Boxes, Bottles, Cans, and Other Persuasive Containers*. Boston: Lit-
           tle, Brown & Co.

Hoshino, K.
   1987   Product conceptualization. In: Jean Umiker-Sebeok (ed.), *Marketing
           and Semiotics*, 41-56. Berlin/New York: Mouton de Gruyter.

Howes, David (ed.)
   1991   *The Varieties of Sensory Experience*. Toronto: University of Toronto
           Press.

Ikuta, Yasutoshi
   1988   *American Romance: The World of Advertising Art*. Tokyo: Heibon-
           sha.

Inglis, F.
   1972   *The Imagery of Power: A Critique of Advertising*. London: Heine-
           mann.

Jacobson, Michael F. and Laurie Ann Mazur
   1995   *Marketing Madness*. Boulder: Westview.

Jakobson, Roman

1960   Linguistics and poetics. In: Thomas A. Sebeok (ed.), *Style and Language*, 34-45. Cambridge, Mass.: MIT Press.

Javed, Naseem

1993   *Naming for Power: Creating Successful Names for the Business World*. Toronto: Linkbridge Publishing.

Jean, Georges

1966   *La poésie*. Paris: Seuil.

Jhally, Sut

1987   *The Codes of Advertising*. New York: St. Martin's Press.

Johnson, Mark

1987   *The Body in the Mind: The Bodily Basis of Meaning, Imagination and Reason*. Chicago: University of Chicago Press.

Jones, John Philip (ed.)

1999   *How to Use Advertising to Build Strong Brands*. London: Sage.

Jung, Carl G.

1956   *Analytical Psychology*. New York: Meridian.

1957   *The Undiscovered Self*. New York: Mentor.

Karmen, Steve

1989   *Through the Jungle: The Art and Business of Making Music for Commercials*. New York: Billboard Books.

Kellner, D.

1995   *Media Culture*. London: Routledge.

Key, Wilson B.

1972   *Subliminal Seduction*. New York: Signet.

1976   *Media Sexploitation*. New York: Signet.

1980   *The Clam-Plate Orgy*. New York: Signet.

1989   *The Age of Manipulation*. New York: Holt.

Kilbourne, J.

1999   *Can't Buy My Love: How Advertising Changes the Way I Feel*. New York: Simon & Schuster.

Klein, Naomi

2000   *No Logo: Taking Aim at the Brand Bullies*. Toronto: Alfred A. Knopf.

Kosslyn, Stephen M.
>   1983   *Ghosts in the Mind's Machine: Creating and Using Images in the Brain*. New York: W. W. Norton.

Krampen, Martin
>   1991   *Children's Drawings: Iconic Coding of the Environment*. New York: Plenum.

Kubey, R. and M. Csikszentmihalyi
>   1990   *Television and the Quality of Life*. Hillsdale, N. J.: Lawrence Erlbaum Associates.

Lakoff, George
>   1987   *Women, Fire and Dangerous Things: What Categories Reveal about the Mind*. Chicago: University of Chicago Press.

Lakoff, George and Mark Johnson
>   1980   *Metaphors We Live By*. Chicago: Chicago University Press.
>   1999   *Philosophy in Flesh: The Embodied Mind and Its Challenge to Western Thought*. New York: Basic.

Lakoff, George and Mark Turner
>   1989   *More than Cool Reason: A Field Guide to Poetic Metaphor*. Chicago: University of Chicago Press.

Langer, Susanne
>   1948   *Philosophy in a New Key*. Cambridge, Mass.: Harvard University Press.

Lasn, Kalle
>   2000   *Culture Jam: The Uncooling of America*. New York: Morrow.

Lefebvre, Henri
>   1968   *La vie quotidienne dans le monde moderne*. Paris: Gallimard.

Leiss, William, Stephen Kline, and Sut Jhally
>   1990   *Social Communication in Advertising: Persons, Products and Images of Well-Being*. Toronto: Nelson.

Leymore, V.
>   1975   *Hidden Myth: Structure and Symbolism in Advertising*. London: Heinemann.

Locke, John
>   1690 [1975]   *An Essay Concerning Human Understanding*, P. H. Nidditch (ed.). Oxford: Clarendon Press.

Lotman, Yuri

  1990   *The Universe of the Mind: A Semiotic Theory of Culture.* Blooming-
          ton: Indiana University Press.

MacCannell, Dean and Jean F. MacCannell

  1982   *The Time of the Sign: A Semiotic Interpretation of Modern Culture.*
          Bloomington: Indiana University Press.

Marchand, R.

  1985   *Advertising the American Dream.: Making the Way for Modernity,
          1920-1940.* Berkeley: University of California Press.

McCracken, Grant

  1988   *Culture and Consumption.* Bloomington: Indiana University Press.

McLuhan, Marshall

  1951   *The Mechanical Bride: Folklore of Industrial Man.* New York: Van-
          guard.

  1962   *The Gutenberg Galaxy.* Toronto: University of Toronto Press.

  1964   *Understanding Media.* London: Routledge and Kegan Paul.

  1972   *Media Ad-Vice.* Englewood Cliffs: Prentice-Hall.

McLuhan, Marshall and Eric McLuhan

  1988   *Laws of Media: The New Science.* Toronto: University of Toronto
          Press.

McNeill, David

  1992   *Hand and Mind: What Gestures Reveal about Thought.* Chicago:
          University of Chicago Press.

Miller, M. C.

  1988   *Boxed In: The Culture of TV.* Evanston: Northwestern University
          Press.

Mittelart, A.

  1991   *Advertising International.* London: Routledge.

Moog, C.

  1990   *Are They Selling Her Lips? Advertising and Identity.* New York:
          Morrow.

Morris, Charles W.

  1946   *Signs, Language and Behavior.* New York: Prentice-Hall.

Myers, G.

    1994   *Words in Ads*. London: Arnold.

Nöth, Winfried

    1990   *Handbook of Semiotics*. Bloomington: Indiana University Press.

O'Barr, William M.

    1994   *Culture and the Ad*. Boulder: Westview Press.

O'Neill-Karch, Mariel

    2000   Medievalism in advertising as value transfer. In: J. Goering and F. Guardiani (eds.), *Medievalism: The Future of the Past*, 11-31. Ottawa: Legas.

Ogden, Charles K. and I. A. Richards

    1923   *The Meaning of Meaning*. London: Routledge and Kegan Paul.

Ortony, Andrew (ed.)

    1979   *Metaphor and Thought*. Cambridge: Cambridge University Press.

Osgood, C. E., G. J. Suci, and P. H. Tannenbaum

    1957   *The Measurement of Meaning*. Urbana: University of Illinois Press.

Packard, Vance

    1957 *The Hidden Persuaders*. New York: McKay.

Panati, Charles

    1984   *Browser's Book of Beginnings*. Boston Houghton Mifflin.

Peirce, Charles S.

    1931-1958 *Collected Papers of Charles Sanders Peirce*, Vols. I-VIII, C. Hartshorne and P. Weiss (eds.). Cambridge, Mass.: Harvard University Press.

Peiss, Kathy

    1998   *Hope in a Jar: The Making of America's Beauty Culture*. New York: Metropolitan Books.

Pollay, R. W.

    1979   *Information Sources in Advertising History*. Westport: Greenwood.

Pollio, H., J. Barlow, H. Fine, and M. Pollio

    1977   *The Poetics of Growth: Figurative Language in Psychology, Psychotherapy, and Education*. Hillsdale, N. J.: Lawrence Erlbaum Associates.

Pope, D.

    1983   *The Making of Modern Advertising*. New York: Basic.

Presbrey, F.

    1968   *The History and Development of Advertising*. Westport: Greenwood.

Reynolds, Richard

    1992   *Super Heroes: A Modern Mythology*. Jackson: University of Mississippi Press.

Reiss, A. and J. Trout

    1981   *Positioning: The Battle for Your Mind*. New York: McGraw-Hill.

Richards, I. A.

    1936   *The Philosophy of Rhetoric*. Oxford: Oxford University Press.

Rossi, William

    1976   *The Sex Lives of the Foot and Shoe*. New York: Dutton.

Rotzoll, K., J. Haefner, and C. Sandage

    1976   *Advertising and Society: Perspectives towards Understanding*. Columbus: Copywright Grid.

Saint-Martin, Fernande

    1990   *Semiotics of Visual Language*. Bloomington: Indiana University Press.

Saussure, Ferdinand de

    1916   *Cours de linguistique générale*. Paris: Payot.

Schank, Roger

    1984   *The Cognitive Computer*. Reading, Mass.: Addison-Wesley.

Scholes, Robert

    1982   *Semiotics and Interpretation*. New Haven: Yale University Press.

Schudson, M.

    1984   *Advertising: The Uneasy Persuasion*. New York: Basic.

Seabrook, J.

    2000   *Nobrow: The Culture of Marketing—The Marketing of Culture*. New York: Knopf.

Sebeok, Thomas A.

    1976   *Contributions to the Doctrine of Signs*. Lanham: University Press of America.

    1979   *The Sign and Its Masters*. Austin: University of Texas Press.

    1981   *The Play of Musement*. Bloomington: Indiana University Press.

1986   *I Think I Am a Verb: More Contributions to the Doctrine of Signs.*
New York: Plenum.

1991   *A Sign is Just a Sign.* Bloomington: Indiana University Press.

1994   *Signs: An Introduction to Semiotics.* Toronto: University of Toronto
Press.

Sebeok, Thomas A. and Marcel Danesi

2000   *The Forms of Meaning: Modeling Systems Theory and Semiotics.*
Berlin/New York: Mouton de Gruyter.

Seiter, Ellen

1987   Semiotics and television. In: Allen Robert Clyde (ed.), *Channels of
Discourse: Television and Contemporary Criticism.*, 17-41. Chapel
Hill: University of North Carolina Press.

Shuker, R.

1994   *Understanding Popular Culture.* London: Routledge.

Silverman, Kaja

1983   *The Subject of Semiotics.* Oxford: Oxford University Press.

Sinclair, J.

1987   *Images Incorporated: Advertising as Industry and Ideology.* Becken-
ham: Croom Helm.

Singer, B.

1986   *Advertising and Society.* Toronto: Addison-Wesley.

Sorgem, Y. K.

1991   Ad games: Postmodern conditions of advertising. *Marketing Signs*
11: 1-15.

Spitzer, L.

1978   La publicité américaine comme art populaire. *Critique* 35: 152-171.

Stark, S.

1997   *Glued to the Set.* New York: Free Press.

Steele, Valerie

1995   *Fetish: Fashion, Sex, and Power.* Oxford: Oxford University Press.

Straubhaar, Joseph and Robert LaRose

2000   *Media Now: Communications Media in the Information Age.* Belmont: Wadsworth.

Tash, Marlene

    1979   Headlines in advertising: The semantics of deviation. *Forum Linguisticum* 3: 222-241.

Thomas, Frank

    1997   *The Conquest of Cool*. Chicago: University of Chicago Press.

Todenhagen, C.

    1999   Advertising in word and image: Textual style and semiotics of English language print advertising. *Zanglist Am* 47: 169-170.

Tuckwell, Keith

    1995   *Advertising in Action*. Englewood Cliffs: Prentice-Hall.

Twitchell, James B.

    2000   *Twenty Ads that Shook the World*. New York: Crown.

Umiker-Sebeok, Jean (ed.)

    1987   *Marketing Signs: New Directions in the Study of Signs for Sale*. Berlin/New York: Mouton de Gruyter.

    1989   Bibliography on semiotic approaches to marketing. *Marketing Signs* 5/6: 1-19.

Umiker-Sebeok, Jean, C. Cossette, and Denis Bachand

    1988   Selected bibliography on the semiotics of marketing. *Semiotic Inquiry* 8: 415-423.

Vardar, N.

    1992   *Global Advertising: Rhyme or Reason?* London: Chapman.

Vestergaard, T. and K. Schrøder

    1985   *The Language of Advertising*. London: Blackwell.

Vygotsky, Lev S.

    1961   *Thought and Language*. Cambridge, Mass.: MIT Press.

Warren, Denise

    1997   Advertising analysis: Cold war versus big thaw vodka advertising. In: Irmengard Rauch and Gerald F. Carr (eds.), *Semiotics around the World: Synthesis in Diversity*, 1251-1254. Berlin/New York: Mouton de Gruyter.

Wernick, Andrew

    1991   *Promotional Culture: Advertising, Ideology, and Symbolic Expression*. London: Gage.

Wheelwright, P.

    1954   *The Burning Fountain: A Study in the Language of Symbolism.* Bloomington: Indiana University Press.

White, R.

    1988   *Advertising: What it Is and How to Do It.* London: McGraw-Hill.

Williamson, Judith

    1978   *Decoding Advertisements: Ideology and Meaning in Advertising.* London: Marion Boyars.

    1985   *Consuming Passions.* London: Marion Boyars.

    1996   But I know what I like: The function of art in advertising. In: Paul Cobley (ed.), *The Communication Reader*, 396-402. London: Routledge.

Wolfe, O.

    1989   Sociosemiology and cross-cultural branding strategies. *Marketing Signs* 3: 3-10.

Woodward, G. C. and R. E. Denton

    1988   *Persuasion and Influence in American Life.* Prospect Heights, Ill.: Waveland.

Index

Made in the USA
Lexington, KY
09 March 2015